BRITISH RAILWAY INFRASTRUCTURE SINCE 1970

AN HISTORICAL OVERVIEW

BRITISH RAILWAY INFRASTRUCTURE SINCE 1970

AN HISTORICAL OVERVIEW

Paul D. Shannon

PEN & SWORD
TRANSPORT

AN IMPRINT OF PEN & SWORD BOOKS LTD.
YORKSHIRE - PHILADELPHIA

First published in Great Britain in 2019 by
Pen and Sword Transport
An imprint of
Pen & Sword Books Ltd
Yorkshire - Philadelphia

ISBN 978 1 52673 479 2

A CIP catalogue record for this book is
available from the British Library.

Typeset by Aura Technology and Software Services, India
Printed and bound in China through Printworks Global Ltd.

Pen & Sword Books Ltd incorporates the Imprints of Pen & Sword
Books Archaeology, Atlas, Aviation, Battleground, Discovery, Family History,
History, Maritime, Military, Naval, Politics, Railways, Select, Transport,
True Crime, Fiction, Frontline Books, Leo Cooper, Praetorian Press,
Seaforth Publishing, Wharncliffe and White Owl.

For a complete list of Pen & Sword titles please contact
PEN & SWORD BOOKS LIMITED
47 Church Street, Barnsley, South Yorkshire, S70 2AS, England
E-mail: enquiries@pen-and-sword.co.uk
Website: www.pen-and-sword.co.uk

or
PEN AND SWORD BOOKS
1950 Lawrence Rd, Havertown, PA 19083, USA
E-mail: Uspen-and-sword@casematepublishers.com
Website: www.penandswordbooks.com

CONTENTS

INTRODUCTION

While the end of regular main-line steam in 1968 was a watershed moment for railway traction, many features of the steam age lived on into the 1970s and beyond. Much of the network was still mechanically signalled; station layouts and buildings were often generous; dozens of small freight terminals and yards remained in place; and the network itself sometimes reflected nineteenth century ownership patterns rather than meeting late twentieth century needs.

By 1970, the cuts proposed in the infamous 1963 report 'The Reshaping of British Railways' – usually known as the Beeching Report – had mostly been resolved one way or another. Many threatened passenger lines and stations had closed, while some had won a long-term reprieve. A relatively small number still hung in the balance, but they included some high-profile cases such as the Settle to Carlisle line and the Kyle of Lochalsh branch. As for freight, BR had succeeded in closing most station goods yards, but private sidings were still numerous and there were still public goods terminals in most major towns.

In the decades since 1970, the railways have seen decline and austerity, but also – especially in recent years – growth and investment. Track layouts were rationalised to take account of streamlined operations and reduced traffic, with less shunting required as both passenger and freight activity shifted towards the unit train concept. But in some cases, the rationalisation went too far: Some station layouts such as those at Oxford and Peterborough proved to be too restrictive once the number of trains began to rise. Some lines were over-hastily singled, only to be returned to double track at great expense, such as Saltney-Rossett in North Wales and Burngullow-Probus in Cornwall.

A number of major towns and cities had fragmented passenger networks which dated back to the ownership patterns of the mid-nineteenth century. Some of these places now benefit from improved connectivity thanks to investment in new cross-city links. Perhaps the best-known example is Thameslink, which restored a main line railway running north to south right through the heart of London. From today's perspective, it seems extraordinary that the line between Farringdon and Blackfriars drifted out of use in 1969 having lost its passenger service decades earlier. The city of Manchester now benefits from two connections – the Windsor link and the Ordsall chord – which improve connectivity between north and south.

Stations have changed in many ways since 1970. Gas lighting was largely phased out in the 1970s, although a few examples lingered into the next decade. Totems in regional colours with matching running-in boards gave way to BR standard signage. Platform buildings were often demolished, especially when stations became unstaffed, and sometimes replaced by basic modular shelters. On the other hand, more attention has been paid to railway heritage. Signal boxes in particular have gained widespread appeal and many have been listed for their historical and architectural merit.

Safety and security occupy a more prominent place than they did forty years ago, and that has affected the look and feel of the railway in various ways. Level crossings of all types have been eliminated where possible, either by means of a costly bridge or underpass or simply by stopping them up and making road users travel further. The work in this area is ongoing and includes the closure of long-standing pedestrian public rights of way across railway lines. Many hundreds of miles of palisade fencing have been erected alongside railways, not just in urban areas but often in remote rural locations. And more and more stations have had ticket barriers installed.

The railway infrastructure of the future is likely to be even more streamlined than that which we know today. Fixed signals may start to disappear as cab signalling becomes more attractive, at least on high-speed lines. The building of HS2 will bring new bridges, cuttings, embankments and above all tunnels to parts of the railway network of the Midlands and Northern England. Urban passenger networks are likely to be developed further through a mixture of heavy rail, light rail and street tramways. Freight facilities are likely to be fewer in number but handling more concentrated traffic volumes as the trend towards longer and heavier trains on core routes continues. While there are many uncertainties, one thing is assured: Our railway will change hugely in the coming decades and sometimes in unpredictable ways, just as it has done since 1970.

CHAPTER 1

THE CHANGING NETWORK

Between 1960 and 1970, the route length covered by British Railways (British Rail from 1965) shrank from just over 18,000 miles to just under 12,000 miles. The cuts hit hardest during the three years after publication of the first Beeching Report; a total of 2,300 miles were chopped from the network in 1964-66. By contrast, the years after 1970 were relatively quiet. The railway still totalled nearly 11,000 miles in 1980 and just under 10,000 miles in 2015.

What those figures do not show is the changing nature of route mileage. Until the 1970s, it was common for secondary lines to lose their passenger service but remain open for freight, either for a specific industry such as a colliery or for general traffic such as goods for export. In some parts of the country such as the South Wales valleys and much of Nottinghamshire, there were more freight-only lines than passenger lines.

Had the recommendations of the 1963 Beeching Report been implemented in full, then the whole of East Lincolnshire south of Grimsby and east of Lincoln would have been left devoid of railways. As it turned out, most of the lines closed in October 1970, but BR retained the meandering route from Grantham to Boston and Skegness, which is still in operation today. The junction station at Firsby was one of the 1970s casualties as it lay on the main line to Grimsby. Standing at the northbound platform in 1970 is a Class 105 DMU in the unusual livery of rail blue with small yellow warning panel. A Class 114 DMU waits in the siding beyond the level crossing. (*Harry Luff/Online Transport Archive*)

The Willoughby-Mablethorpe branch succumbed in October 1970 along with the demise of the main line to Grimsby. Two Class 114 units are pictured at Willoughby during its final year of operation. The station had retained its full track layout to the end, with a generous double junction linking the main line with the Mablethorpe branch and even a run round loop for the side platform. The goods yard, however, had closed in 1966. (*Harry Luff/Online Transport Archive*)

The border town of Oswestry had lost its passenger services in 1966, but the goods yard remained open until December 1971 and ballast trains from Blodwell continued to pass through the site until 1989. The photograph dated September 1971 hints at the one-time importance of Oswestry as a railway centre, with the former Cambrian Railways headquarters still standing on the northbound platform. Out of sight beyond the station lay the former Cambrian Railways locomotive and wagon works. The semaphore signals had been removed after the closure of Oswestry South box in November 1970. (*Marcus Eavis/Online Transport Archive*)

Typical of the dozens of small lines that owed their existence to specific industries, the Brymbo branch in North Wales remained busy with traffic between Croes Newydd yard and Brymbo steelworks throughout the 1970s. Class 24 5035 passes Brymbo East box with empty hoppers in this scene from June 1973. By the end of the decade, the branch service was down to two trains a day and further reductions in business would make its retention unviable. It closed in October 1982. The steelworks itself survived until 1990. (*R.W.A. Jones/Online Transport Archive*)

Having unsurprisingly been targeted for closure in the 1963 Beeching Report, the Alston branch then survived for more than a decade until the local road network had been improved to support a replacement bus service. The branch eventually closed in May 1976, having been worked as a long siding from Haltwhistle in its later years. A Class 108 DMU is pictured at the terminus on 20 March 1976. Part of the branch trackbed has subsequently returned to railway use thanks to the two-foot gauge South Tynedale Railway, which runs between Alston and Slaggyford. (*Paul Shannon*)

London's City Widened Lines enabled main line trains from the Midland and Great Northern commuter routes to reach Moorgate in the heart of the city. Trains ran in the peak hours only and were a mixture of DMUs and rakes of hauled non-corridor stock hauled by Class 31s. One of the latter workings calls at Farringdon in September 1976. The Great Northern trains were withdrawn two months later, while those from the Midland continued until 1979, when the line was severed beyond Farringdon to allow the construction of Thameslink. (*Marcus Eavis/Online Transport Archive*)

The two-mile line from Dalston Junction into London Broad Street was once busy enough to justify six tracks, four of which remained in use into the 1970s. By that time, the line was used mainly by the 20-minute interval electric service to Richmond, plus peak hour trains to Watford Junction and various stations on the Great Northern line via Finsbury Park. A Class 116 DMU calls at Dalston Junction on a Great Northern service in February 1977. The line through Dalston Junction closed in 1986 when the last peak hour trains to Watford were withdrawn, the Richmond service having already been diverted away in the previous year. However, tracks were later relaid on this alignment as part of the East London line extension. (*Marcus Eavis/Online Transport Archive*)

Wombwell marked the start of the seven-mile Worsborough incline, which included a three-mile stretch with an average gradient of 1 in 40. The line was electrified in the 1950s as part of the Woodhead scheme. Loaded trains generally required a pair of Class 76 bankers from Wombwell to West Silkstone. Passing Wombwell Main Junction box on 15 April 1980 are 76036 and 76039 with a diverted mixed freight from Tinsley to Dewsnap. The Worsborough incline closed along with the Woodhead route on 20 July 1981 and Wombwell Main Junction box was abolished in February 1982, leaving the remaining route through Wombwell open for a little longer to serve Barrow colliery. (*Paul Shannon*)

Both Lincoln's passenger stations – Central and St Marks – suffered from the inconvenience of a city centre level crossing. The unusual track layout at St Marks with two dead-end sidings between the through lines is pictured on 5 June 1980, as a three-car Class 120 DMU stands at the eastbound platform on a service from Nottingham. BR closed St Marks and its level crossing in May 1985 after completing an 80-metre curve to connect the Nottingham line with the former Lincoln avoiding line, allowing Nottingham trains to call at Lincoln Central instead. (*Paul Shannon*)

An unusual situation arose at New Holland where two 'stations' – Town and Pier – were connected by a single platform. On 5 June 1980, a Class 105 unit arrives at New Holland Town on the branch train to Barton-on-Humber, while a Class 114 unit waits at New Holland Pier with a service to Cleethorpes. The pier lost its passenger purpose with the opening of the Humber Road Bridge, and BR replaced both New Holland stations in June 1981 with a single wooden platform served by direct trains from Cleethorpes to Barton-on-Humber. The track to the pier was retained for occasional freight use until 1998. (*Paul Shannon*)

In its later years, the Consett branch in County Durham owed its existence to Consett steel works, which took in iron ore and other raw materials by rail as well as sending out finished products. Ingots and fuel oil are among the traffic types pictured here at Consett in June 1980. The works would close just three months later with the loss of around 3,000 jobs. The branch line kept going after the works closure to remove scrap metal and other materials from the site as well as for deliveries of household coal, but it carried its last ever train – a railtour organised by the Derwentside Rail Action Group – on 17 March 1984. Today, the trackbed forms part of the Coast to Coast cycle route. (*Michael Rhodes*)

The Clayton West branch was reprieved from the Beeching list in 1966 but then lived a precarious existence with little investment and a gradual run-down of facilities. Clayton West station was gas lit until 1968 and became unstaffed in 1970. A Class 101 DMU stands at Clayton West on 7 January 1981, ready to return to Huddersfield. By that time, closure was again being mooted and indeed passenger services on the branch were eventually withdrawn in January 1983. The track was then left in place for coal traffic from Emley Moor colliery, adjacent to Skelmanthorpe station, but that too ceased before long and tracklifting began in 1986. Today, the Kirklees Light Railway runs a 15-inch gauge line over part of the trackbed from Clayton West to Shelley. (*Paul Shannon*)

Forfar once lay on the Caledonian Railway main line from Perth to Aberdeen, but in September 1967 it lost its passenger services and became the end of a 26-mile freight-only branch from Stanley Junction. Coal, potatoes, timber, fertiliser and agricultural lime provided enough traffic for a regular branch train from Perth yard throughout the 1970s. An ancient crane overlooks the partly derelict yard at Forfar on 23 March 1981 as 27023 shunts vans from the morning arrival. This old-style wagonload operation did not last much longer; the branch closed to all traffic on 7 June 1982. (*Paul Shannon*)

Since the 1980s, the trend has reversed. Some lines have become passenger-only after losing their last source of freight. The number of freight-only lines has shrunk due to the closure of collieries, steelworks and other industrial sites. Some former freight-only lines have closed completely while others have become passenger-only lines, either with or without a break in usage. And, where completely new lines have been built, such as the Channel Tunnel Rail Link (HS1), the main target has been passenger traffic.

Many, but not all, of the passenger closures of the 1970s were lines recommended for closure in 'The Reshaping of British Railways'. Between 1970 and 1976 the casualties included a number of rural and secondary routes such as the

Hayfield branch, Rose Hill-Macclesfield, the Caernarvon (now Caernarfon) branch, Lowestoft-Yarmouth, Bridgend-Maesteg, Rochdale-Bury-Bolton, Bury-Rawtenstall, the Ilfracombe branch, the Bridport branch, Cambridge-St Ives, the Minehead branch, Penrith-Keswick, Alton-Winchester, the Newcastle Riverside branch, Liverpool-Gateacre, the Alston branch, and most lines in East Lincolnshire.

Some of those lines had been proposed for closure a long time earlier. The Alston branch, for example, had been under threat since the 1950s and had been reduced to a single track 'siding' from Haltwhistle in the early 1960s in an effort to stem losses and keep the service going. Its demise was delayed until 1976 because it took a long time to improve the local road network for a replacement bus service.

Addiscombe was a small suburban terminus not far from the centre of Croydon. It lost its through trains from London in 1950 and was then served by a shuttle from Elmers End. Class 416 unit 5714 stands at the terminus with the shuttle on 10 June 1981. Passenger numbers continued to decline and by 1993, the booking office was staffed at peak hours only. Complete closure came on 2 June 1997, the last train having been an enthusiasts' special on 31 May. Part of the branch has since been incorporated into Croydon Tramlink and the site of Addiscombe station is now occupied by housing. (*Paul Shannon*)

Around Mansfield, many miles of railway existed purely for coal. Some lines had once carried passengers and general freight, but others had always been colliery branches. In the heart of the maze of freight-only lines lay Mansfield Concentration Sidings, where shunters 08429 and 08266 are seen in action on 15 June 1981. The sidings at that time were still gathering wagonload coal traffic from some of the local pits, but that practice would not last much longer as more and more traffic switched to trainload merry-go-round operation. The signal box that controlled Mansfield Concentration Sidings closed in July 1986 and the line gradually became less busy as one by one the collieries succumbed; the last recorded movement past this location took place in June 2003. (*Paul Shannon*)

The 'new' Woodhead Tunnel had a working life of just 28 years. A combination of non-standard electrification and falling traffic led BR to close the Woodhead route in July 1981. Passenger trains on the central section between Hadfield and Penistone had already been withdrawn in 1970 and it was relatively easy for BR to divert the remaining freight flows - mainly coal from Yorkshire to Fiddlers Ferry power station. On 19 June 1981 76038 and 76039 emerge light engine from the west end of the tunnel, probably heading for Godley Junction to collect a rake of empty merry-go-round hoppers. On the left are the bores of the original Woodhead Tunnels, which had carried trains for almost a century but were unsuitable for electrification. (*Paul Shannon*)

The March to Spalding line was not targeted for closure in the 1963 Beeching Report. It formed part of a useful route for freight which would otherwise have had to compete with express passenger trains on the East Coast main line, and it carried a modest amount of passenger traffic, including the Harwich-Manchester 'North Country Continental' boat train until May 1973. A pair of Class 25s, 25032 and 25286, passes one of the intermediate boxes on the line at Cowbit on 20 June 1981. With freight traffic in decline, BR decided to close the March-Spalding line and its demise took effect on 1 November 1982. In recent years, the need for a freight alternative to the East Coast main line has been felt again, but the March-Spalding line will not reopen; instead Network Rail is building a dive-under line at Werrington Junction to enable trains to run from March to Spalding via Peterborough without conflicting with the East Coast line. (*Paul Shannon*)

An intricate network of lines served the collieries and other industries around Staveley in North Nottinghamshire. Seymour Junction lay at the divergence of the former Midland Railway line to Pleasley, which had closed as a through route in the 1930s and latterly served Markham and Bolsover collieries, and the line to Elmton & Creswell via Clowne which lasted as a through route until the 1990s. Seymour Junction box opened in 1963 and closed in 2006 after the end of coal traffic from Oxcroft disposal point. 20023 and 20001 pull a heavy rake of mineral wagons out of the sidings on 27 July 1981. (*Paul Shannon*)

Kilmacolm became a terminus in operational terms when the through line to Greenock lost its local passenger service in 1959. The route beyond Kilmacolm closed completely in 1966, after which time the remaining branch from Elderslie was singled. BR continued to run a Glasgow-Kilmacolm service via Paisley Canal, but this was withdrawn on 10 January 1983. Signs of dereliction are already apparent as a Class 116 DMU waits to depart from Kilmacolm on 29 August 1981. The trackbed between Elderslie and Kilmacolm later became part of the National Cycle Network. (*Paul Shannon*)

The Leamside line from Pelaw to Tursdale lost its regular passenger services in stages between 1941 and 1964 but remained a useful freight and diversionary route in the diesel era. Part of the route was used by the heavy iron ore trains from Redcar to Consett, which reversed direction at Washington. As regular traffic declined, retention of the line became harder to justify and it was mothballed as a through route in May 1991, with just a short stretch remaining in use between Pelaw and Wardley for opencast coal. Since 1991, there has been much talk of reopening the Leamside line and bridges and other structures have been left in place for that eventuality. On 5 November 1981, 46049 passes the unusual North Eastern Railway box at Penshaw North with a train comprising 62 empty mineral wagons. (*Paul Shannon*)

In the early 1980s, numerous colliery branches still traced the valleys running north from Newport, Cardiff, Tondu and Neath. The Tondu area was particularly interesting, as Tondu was the meeting place for two routes from the south – from Bridgend and Margam – and four separate branches to the north and east – to Maesteg, Garw, Ogmore and Raglan. 37178 drifts down the Garw branch on 15 April 1982 with coal for Ogmore Valley washery in the next valley. The train would run round in the loop just north of Tondu station. The last train of freshly mined coal from Garw ran in 1986, but the branch was later temporarily reopened for a flow of reclaimed coal from 1995 until March 1997. Since then, a short stretch of the former railway has been restored as a museum line. (*Paul Shannon*)

The Weardale branch from Bishop Auckland to Eastgate carried cement traffic until March 1993, some 30 years after the withdrawal of passenger services. In later years, the cement was bound mainly for Middlesbrough and Heaton on Tyneside. 37172 passes Wolsingham box with train 6K70 to Heaton on 24 May 1982. The box closed in June 1983, when one train working was introduced between Bishop Auckland and Eastgate. After the cement traffic had finished, the track was left in place and work was carried out to enable a heritage passenger services to start running. Today, the Weardale Railway runs a summer service between Bishop Auckland and Stanhope, calling at Wolsingham and two other stations. The line also enjoyed a freight revival from 2011 until 2013, when Colas Rail hauled trainloads of opencast coal from Wolsingham to Scunthorpe and Ratcliffe. (*Paul Shannon*)

The four-track formation at Cudworth points to the heavy freight and passenger traffic that once used the ex-Midland Railway main line between Wath Road Junction and Goose Hill Junction. The line had closed to scheduled passenger traffic in 1968, mainly because mining subsidence limited the speed of express trains. It regained some Sheffield-Leeds trains in 1973, but as there were no intermediate stations it was vulnerable and it closed permanently as a through route in June 1987, with just the section from Cudworth to Oakenshaw Junction remaining open for freight. On 1 June 1982, 56089 passes the site of Cudworth station with a merry-go-round coal train from Grimethorpe. Today, a single track survives at this location to carry trainloads of silica sand to Monk Bretton. (*Paul Shannon*)

While most of the delayed Beeching closures were total, a few of the former mixed traffic lines remained open for freight. The Maesteg line was kept alive by coal traffic; the Rochdale-Bury-Rawtenstall route continued to handle a weekly train of domestic coal; and in East Lincolnshire freight traffic remained on the Peterborough-Spalding, Grimsby-Louth and Lincoln-Bardney lines. Parts of the Cambridge-St Ives, Newcastle Riverside and Liverpool-Gateacre lines were also retained for freight.

A small number of lines lost their passenger service in the first half of the 1970s despite not appearing in the 1963 Beeching Report. The most prominent example was the Woodhead route, which as late as 1965 had been earmarked for development in preference to other trans-Pennine lines. In the end, it was the need to replace non-standard electrification and life-expired signalling which swayed the decision against Woodhead; it lost its through passenger services in 1970 and the central section closed completely in 1981. Conversely, the once threatened Hope Valley line was reprieved and took most of the passenger traffic that was formerly routed via Woodhead – as well as trains between Manchester and Derby which had previously used the Midland route via Matlock.

The Fleetwood branch and Skipton-Colne were further examples of casualties not foreseen in the 1963 Report. Fleetwood continued to handle freight for a time, but the closure of Skipton-Colne was complete.

The single-platform terminus at Bodmin General closed to passengers in 1967, but the line and run-round loop were retained for freight traffic to Wadebridge and Wenford Bridge. The Wadebridge line closed in 1978, while china clay trains from Wenford Bridge continued until September 1983. With the station buildings remarkably intact after 15 years of disuse, 37299 has just run round its train of 'clay hoods' returning empty to Wenford Bridge on 3 August 1982. After the china clay trains finished, North Cornwall District Council secured the trackbed and the Bodmin Railway Preservation Society was able to set about reopening the line as a heritage railway. Regular services began from Bodmin Road to Bodmin General in 1990 and were extended from Bodmin General to Boscarne Junction in 1996. (*Paul Shannon*)

The Wirksworth branch on the fringe of the Derbyshire Peak District closed to regular passenger services as early as 1947. The quarries in and around Wirksworth continued to keep the branch alive until December 1989, with seasonal trains of sugar stone forming the last revenue-earning traffic. 31293 stands in the 'dust dock' siding on 15 April 1983 with tippler wagons that were being loaded with limestone dust for use as a flux in the steelmaking industry. The generous track layout had been essentially unchanged for decades. After closure, the Wirksworth branch was quickly earmarked as a potential heritage railway and today the Ecclesbourne Valley Railway Association runs seasonal trains over the whole line between Duffield and Wirksworth. (*Paul Shannon*)

Tunbridge Wells West was the main intermediate station on the Tunbridge Wells Central to Eridge line, which was proposed for closure in the 1963 Beeching Report but survived – albeit with minimal investment – for another 20 years. Class 207 DEMU 1305 enters Tunbridge Wells West station with a train from Eridge on 23 August 1983. The semaphore gantry was not the station's only relic from a bygone age; more remarkably, the booking hall was still gas lit in the 1980s. With the track and signalling in need of unaffordable replacement, BR finally closed the line in July 1985. The Tunbridge Wells and Eridge Railway Preservation Society was then formed and restored a limited passenger service, which became the Spa Valley Railway and was extended to Eridge in 2011. (*Paul Shannon*)

The line from Skelton Junction to Latchford near Warrington lost its regular passenger service in 1962 but continued to form part of the important freight corridor from Yorkshire to Merseyside via Woodhead. A Hertfordshire Railtours special from London St Pancras to Amlwch crosses the Manchester Ship Canal just east of Latchford on 10 December 1983, hauled by 45111. By that time, freight via Skelton Junction and Latchford had diminished greatly and the bridge needed expensive repairs; the line closed completely in July 1985. All surviving freight could be diverted either via Chat Moss and Warrington Bank Quay or via Northwich. (*Paul Shannon*)

Although most light rail systems operate completely independently from the main-line railway, there have been and still are exceptions. Until the 1980s, BR used Tyne & Wear Metro tracks to reach the Rowntrees distribution terminal at Coxlodge, north of Newcastle. 31178 propels one VDA van with attendant brake van into the Rowntrees siding on 20 February 1984, having worked trip 9P03 from Tyne Yard. This traffic ceased when Rowntrees pulled out of rail in 1987. Today, although freight no longer works over Metro tracks, Metro trains share the Network Rail line between Pelaw and Sunderland. (*Paul Shannon*)

Nine and a half miles of the former Rugby to Leamington Spa line together with a short stretch of the former Marton Junction to Weedon line were retained to provide access to the Rugby Cement works at Southam. On 9 April 1984, 25175 arrives at Marton Junction with empty mineral wagons from the cement works, having just traversed the section from Southam which diverges to the right in this photograph. Towering above the railway is a structure which when completed in 1851 was the longest single-span wrought iron bridge of its kind in existence; it was strengthened in later years by additional lattice columns and cross ties. The 1984/85 miners' strike rapidly brought the coal traffic to a standstill and the branch was officially closed in August 1985. (*Paul Shannon*)

Despite not figuring in the 1963 Beeching Report, the Wymondham-Dereham-Kings Lynn line closed to passengers in 1968/69. The section from Wymondham to Dereham was retained for freight along with the line from Dereham to Fakenham, which had closed to passengers in 1964. The track was cut back from Fakenham to Great Ryburgh in August 1980 and to North Elmham shortly afterwards. The traffic was mainly grain from North Elmham, but Dereham also received fertiliser by rail. The line had many unstaffed level crossing gates and when trains ran beyond North Elmham, the out and back journey from Norwich took too long to be covered in a single shift, requiring a change of crew en route. On 17 April 1984, 31109 comes off the branch at Wymondham with two Polybulk wagons for Burton-on-Trent. The branch closed to regular freight in 1989 but remained connected to the network and carried occasional military loads; in recent times the Mid-Norfolk Railway Preservation Trust has established a successful heritage operation from Dereham. (*Paul Shannon*)

The Associated Octel plant at Amlwch kept the 17-mile Gaerwen to Amlwch branch open for nearly three decades after its closure to passengers in 1964. 47128 poses just outside the plant, on the short stretch of light railway that was built in 1952, ready to depart with train 7D05, the 0825 to Llandudno Junction, on 18 April 1985. The payload includes four ethylene dibromide tanks and four liquid chlorine tanks, all bound for Ellesmere Port. The Associated Octel plant stopped using rail in 1993 at a time when people were becoming more aware of the dangers of moving a large quantity of chemicals in one unit. Since then, proposals have been made both to convert the trackbed into a cycle route and to restore it as a passenger railway. In 2012, volunteers from Lein Amlwch gained a licence from Network Rail to start clearing the overgrown track with a view to its eventual reopening. (*Paul Shannon*)

Molasses traffic to Menstrie kept part of the Stirling to Alloa line alive until 1993. The molasses trains used to run round in Alloa yard, but the opening of a run round loop at Cambus enabled the closure of the stretch between Cambus and Alloa in December 1987. 27063 is pictured with molasses tanks at Cambus Junction on 20 July 1984. When that traffic finished, the Stirling to Cambus line was mothballed, later to be revived as part of the ambitious Stirling-Alloa-Kincardine reopening project. Passenger services through Cambus resumed in May 2008 and the line was also used by coal trains to Longannet until the power station closed in March 2016. (*Paul Shannon*)

The rail network in West Wales received a boost when branch lines opened to serve three oil refineries: Herbrandston in 1960; Waterston in 1968; and Robeston in 1973. For just over a decade, all three refineries distributed some of their oil by rail. Herbrandston was the first to close, with the last train running in January 1984. The demise of Waterston followed in December 1984, and Robeston stopped refining in November 2014, although it was then sold to Puma Energy as has remained active as a storage and distribution terminal. Most trains from the refineries departed at night, but 47032 is pictured leaving Waterston with the daytime 6M50 train to West Bromwich Albion on 10 July 1985. (*Paul Shannon*)

The Selby diversion was the first stretch of railway in the UK to be built with a design speed of 125mph. As well as making it possible to mine coal beneath the old line from Selby to York, the new line neatly avoided the 40mph speed restriction over Selby swing bridge. Opening took place in stages, with the section north of Hambleton carrying Hull-York trains from May 1983 and the remaining section from Temple Hirst Junction to Hambleton following on 30 September 1983. An InterCity 125 unit with 43175 leading passes Hambleton South Junction with an up express on 20 July 1985. (*Paul Shannon*)

A short stretch of the Longridge branch in Lancashire remained open to serve Deepdale coal depot, which became one of the last few domestic coal depots to survive on BR. The coal came from various locations in South Wales and Yorkshire. 20094 and 20080 are in charge of the trip working from Warrington Arpley to Deepdale on 2 August 1985, negotiating the litter-strewn track on the approach to the terminal. From 1986, Deepdale was served by a direct train from Healey Mills and this in turn was later replaced by a service from South Wales. The coal traffic ceased in 1994 and the track quickly became unusable. (*Paul Shannon*)

Although the freight scene in County Durham was dominated by coal, several branches and terminals served limestone quarries which produced industrial dolomite and agricultural lime. In the Ferryhill area, traffic was forwarded from Thrislington works and from a loading pad at Ferryhill itself, while short branch lines served quarries at Coxhoe and Raisby Hill. 37058 waits at Raisby Hill with a short rake of MTV wagons on 1 November 1985. By that time the Coxhoe branch had already been disconnected from the main line and the Raisby Hill branch would soon fall into disuse. (*Paul Shannon*)

The Oldham loop was spared in the 1963 Beeching Report, but the line came close to being truncated when in 1972, the Secretary of State for Transport announced permission to withdraw services between Oldham Mumps and Rochdale. That threat was lifted by the promise of a subsidy from SELNEC - later to become the Greater Manchester Passenger Transport Executive. However, the long-term future of the line was only safe once it was decided to incorporate it into the Metrolink light rail network. Initial proposals for light rail to Rochdale had been made in the 1980s, but it was not until 2009 that the line closed for conversion. Its reopening took place in stages between 2011 and 2014. Back in BR days, a Class 142 'Pacer' unit in original Greater Manchester livery arrives at Oldham Mumps on 8 March 1986. (*Paul Shannon*)

In the south, the Okehampton and Swanage branches succumbed, although the rails through Okehampton remained in regular use for ballast from Meldon quarry and part of the Swanage branch remained in use for oil and clay from Furzebrook.

From 1977 until 1990, the pace of passenger line closures slowed. On Tyneside, the South Shields branch and the Tynemouth loop lost their BR service, but both lines would later be reopened as part of the Tyne & Wear Metro. The former Midland main line through Cudworth was downgraded and eventually closed, but no stations were affected and trains were simply diverted via Moorthorpe. Elsewhere in Yorkshire, both the Huddersfield-Penistone-Sheffield line and its offshoot to Clayton West were repeatedly threatened, but only the Clayton West branch actually closed.

In Scotland, the Glasgow-Paisley Canal-Kilmacolm line had been under threat since the 1960s and finally closed in 1983. In London and the South East, two potential closures from the Beeching era came to delayed fruition: Woodside-Selsdon-Sanderstead closed in 1983 and Tunbridge Wells-Eridge in 1985.

The list of BR freight-only lines became significantly shorter between 1970 and 1990. In the South West, the branches to Wadebridge and Wenford Bridge were axed, in the latter case bringing to an end a complex operation involving two run-round movements and the use of a Class 08 shunter for part of the journey. In South Wales, the freight-only route mileage shrank as collieries closed; among the more significant losses were the four branches from Tondu – although the Maesteg line later

Once a main line, the Cheshire Lines Committee route into Liverpool Central High Level closed to passengers in April 1972, having carried only a local service from Gateacre in its later years. Freight lasted a little longer, with oil trains from Brunswick occasionally shining the rails until the mid-1970s. The intermediate passenger stations were left intact and the line was reopened in January 1978 when the electrified tracks from Southport were extended via Liverpool Central Low Level to Garston. A further extension to Hunts Cross was completed in 1983. Unit 507020 calls at Cressington with a train for Hunts Cross on 2 April 1986. (*Paul Shannon*)

To the east of Stoke-on-Trent, two freight only branches survived into the 1980s, serving the Tarmac quarry at Cauldon Low and British Industrial Sand at Oakamoor. The two branches met at Leek Brook Junction. On 27 August 1986, 20121 and 20188 pass the preserved station at Cheddleton with the 1005 St Helens-Oakamoor sand empties. These air-braked hoppers had replaced older rolling stock in 1986. The last sand train from Oakamoor ran on 30 August 1988 and the branch was officially closed on 17 May 1993. Since then, the Churnet Valley Railway has restored Cheddleton station to its former glory as well as introducing heritage trains along part of the Oakamoor branch. (*Paul Shannon*)

reopened to passengers, as well as the Maerdy branch, and the branches to Blaenavon and Hafodyrynys on the eastern fringe of the coalfield.

It was a similar story in the East Midlands coalfield. The plethora of lines around Mansfield was progressively thinned as a result of mining cutbacks. The Mansfield area network in 1970 had been particularly intricate, with several collieries enjoying separate main line connections from former Midland Railway and former Great Central routes. And in North East England, many colliery lines closed, some owned by BR and others by the National Coal Board. Coal was not the only industry whose decline caused a pruning of the rail freight network. A significant closure was the Consett branch, very busy in the 1970s but surplus to requirements after Consett steelworks closed.

Through freight-only lines were vulnerable where their traffic could be diverted to other routes. In the West Midlands, the South Staffordshire line from Lichfield to Walsall closed as a through route in 1984, with the Walsall-Round Oak section following suit in 1993. In the

East Midlands, the closure of the High Marnham-Lincoln line in 1980 was barely noticed because its traffic could easily be diverted via Gainsborough. In North West England, the Skelton Junction-Warrington line lost much of its business after the demise of Woodhead and closed in 1985. The South Manchester loop from Trafford Park to Gorton was deemed to be dispensable, although in this instance its retention might have helped to overcome the twenty-first century congestion through Manchester Oxford Road. In Scotland, the Dunfermline-Alloa-Stirling and Bathgate-Airdrie lines closed to through traffic.

Rural freight-only branches were already a rarity in 1970, and those that remained were vulnerable unless they produced a large and steady volume of traffic. The casualties in Southern England, with their last traffic flows in brackets, included Abingdon (coal), Wallingford (grain), Chinnor (coal), Hemel Hempstead Hemelite branch (clinker ash), Dunstable (cement and oil) and Southam (coal). In East Anglia, the last remnant of the Fakenham branch closed, as did the meandering route from Wroxham to Lenwade via the 1960 Themelthorpe curve.

The Ebbw Vale branch was by no means the only railway line to pass through three distinct phases – passenger and freight, then freight only, then passenger only. The original passenger service ceased in April 1962, but the line remained busy with steel and other freight to and from Ebbw Vale steelworks as well as coal from several pits along the valley. Steel making at Ebbw Vale ended in 1975 but the works remained open for finishing and tinplate manufacturing. A new set of sidings was provided at Ebbw Vale in 1989, by which time the traffic consisted of incoming steel coil from Llanwern and Port Talbot and outgoing tinplate for Worcester, Wisbech and Westhoughton. A trainload of hot rolled coil arrives at the new yard on 2 May 1995 headed by a Transrail-liveried Class 60 loco. The works closed completely in 2002, with the last train running in July of that year. Fortunately, the track was left in place; the third phase of the line's existence began in February 2008 when passenger services were restored to Ebbw Vale Parkway. An extension to Ebbw Vale Town followed in May 2015. (*Michael Rhodes*)

Freight lines that do not serve a specific customer are always vulnerable. Following the run-down of local traffic, the Round Oak-Walsall line in the West Midlands carried only through trains, which could be diverted over other routes. 47218 passes Wednesbury with 6M72, the 2200 St Blazey to Cliffe Vale train, on 22 May 1987. At that time, this train was a Speedlink wagonload working and, although it existed mainly for china clay to Cliffe Vale, it could carry other flows as required. The Round Oak-Walsall line closed in March 1993, but the formation has been protected and the West Midlands Metro hopes to run trams over the stretch between Wednesbury and Brierley Hill by 2022. (*Paul Shannon*)

The Dee Marsh Junction to Mickle Trafford line closed to passengers in October 1969 and to freight in May 1984. However, the singling of the Chester to Wrexham line created pathing difficulties for steel trains between Ravenscraig and Dee Marsh Junction, and this prompted the reopening of a single track between Dee Marsh Junction and Mickle Trafford in August 1986. Passing Sealand on the revived route on 17 October 1987 are 20154 and 20009 with empty steel carriers returning to Ravenscraig. After the closure of Ravenscraig, the line through Sealand was again declared surplus and it carried its last revenue-earning train in July 1992. (*Paul Shannon*)

The Heathfield branch in Devon had been freight-only since 1959 and still generated several types of freight in the 1980s, including ball clay, oil and occasional deliveries of animal feed. Railfreight Distribution-liveried loco 37673 couples up to a single clay wagon in the loading terminal on 19 February 1988, ready to return to St Blazey yard. The ball clay continued until the early 1990s, while the oil trains from Waterston finished in December 1995 in favour of deliveries to Plymouth by coastal shipping. But that was not quite the end; the line was reopened in December 2011 to load timber from a lineside pad at Teigngrace, which lasted until early 2015. (*Paul Shannon*)

A resurgence in opencast coal from Ayrshire brought several railway revivals in the 1980s. One was the reopening in March 1988 of the line between Annbank and Mauchline, which had closed three years earlier at the time of the Ayrshire resignalling scheme. The reopened line provided a shorter route for coal trains from Knockshinnoch to Ayr Harbour which would otherwise have to run via Kilmarnock. On 3 April 1989, 20206 and 37374 pass Annbank with 7R04 from Knockshinnoch to Ayr Harbour. Diverging to the right is the Killoch branch, which also saw an increase in traffic. (*Paul Shannon*)

An unlikely freight survivor in an inner city environment was the Silvertown Tramway, reached by a spur from the North Woolwich branch. In its last years, the line served just one scrapyard, which forwarded traffic to Aldwarke in South Yorkshire. A trip working ran as required from Temple Mills yard, connecting with the Speedlink wagonload network. 37087 propels two POA scrap carriers towards the scrapyard on 4 July 1989. The operation would soon come to an end and the Silvertown Tramway was officially closed in June 1991. The line from Stratford to North Woolwich closed in 2006, but much of the trackbed now forms a branch of the Docklands Light Railway. (*Paul Shannon*)

In Manchester, the building of the Windsor Link helped to overcome the long-standing north-south split, making it possible for trains from Preston and Bolton to run directly into Manchester Oxford Road and Piccadilly. The Windsor Link carried through trains between Blackpool and East Anglia from May 1988, with other services following in May 1989. 31468 takes the new route at Ordsall Lane Junction with a train for the Bolton direction on 6 September 1989. Just to the right of the locomotive are the tracks of the Chat Moss line to Liverpool, while the sidings further on the right served a distribution terminal. (*Paul Shannon*)

In Lincolnshire, the Louth and Bardney lines carried their last trains of grain and sugar beet respectively. In northern England, freight-only closures included the Rawtenstall branch, the remaining lines running inland from Corkickle in West Cumbria, the Warcop branch from Appleby, and the Callerton branch in Northumberland. In Scotland, the branches to Forfar, Brechin, Fraserburgh and Dufftown were all erased from the freight-only map.

Alongside the line closures, the two decades from 1970 to 1990 saw an increasing number of line reopenings – and in a few cases the building of entirely new lines. Almost all were for passengers, but a small number targeted specific freight flows, such as the Drax branch which reopened in 1972 for power station coal and the Boulby branch which was restored for potash and rock salt.

One of the first post-Beeching passenger line revivals was the return of a limited service between Peterborough and Spalding in June 1971. A subsidy from Lincolnshire County Council and South Holland District Council allowed BR to run two return trips each weekday on the line, with a third train on certain Saturdays. The reintroduced service was continuously under review, but eventually it became part of the national network – especially after the closure of the March-Spalding line in 1982.

Even while the Beeching Report was still a recent memory, the appetite for reopening closed lines grew rapidly. Numerous appeals and campaigns were made, some more realistic than others. Among the reopening aspirations in the 1970s were Uckfield-Lewes, Guildford-Cranleigh, Hoo Junction-Grain, Wymondham-Fakenham, King's Lynn-Hunstanton, Barry-Bridgend, Stourbridge Junction-Dudley

A controversial line closure was the St Ives branch in Cambridgeshire. Passenger services ceased in October 1970 and the long-standing sand traffic from Fen Drayton to London King's Cross switched to road transport in May 1992. There had also been a small-scale flow of imported fruit to Histon until 1983. After closure, Cambridgeshire County Council proposed reopening the line to passengers and that campaign was later taken up by the group Cast.iron. However, in the end the Council opted instead to convert the route into a guided busway, which opened in 2011. One of the last passenger specials on the line, organised by the Railway Development Society, passes Histon on 24 March 1990. (*Paul Shannon*)

The Trafford Park Estates Railway bucked a national trend when several of its tramway-style lines reopened for business in 1989. The company upgraded its track to take modern wagons and acquired two Class 08 locomotives from BR to haul trains to and from the exchange sidings. The first two customers were Norton Metals, who dispatched scrap metal to Cardiff, and Cerestar, who forwarded starch to Kent and Scotland. Ex-BR loco 08669 mingles with road traffic as it hauls empty scrap carriers along one of the estate lines on 6 July 1990. The railway remained in use for another decade after this photograph. (*Paul Shannon*)

and Colne-Skipton. Some of those aspirations have been fulfilled, some are ongoing battles in the twenty-first century and some have been abandoned.

In urban areas, the formation of Passenger Transport Executives from 1969 onwards encouraged the expansion of the rail network. Merseyside benefited from two new rail tunnels in the late 1970s, allowing the integration of Wirral line services with those on the lines that formerly radiated from Liverpool Exchange and Central stations. One part of this ambitious project was the reopening of the former Cheshire Lines route through Garston. In Strathclyde, the reopening of the line from Partick to Rutherglen via Queen Street Low Level was a major step towards improving Glasgow's commuter network. In London – not a PTE area as such – the return of passenger trains to the Dalston-Stratford route in 1979 marked the beginning of a new era for the North London line.

Reopenings in less densely populated areas in the 1970s included the return of passenger trains to the Ladybank-Perth line, the reopening of the Leamington Spa-Coventry line for InterCity trains and the revival

of trains to Sinfin near Derby. The Sinfin project was one of the few reopenings that failed; the service did not attract sufficient custom and was eventually withdrawn in 1993.

In the 1980s, the biggest network enhancement was the opening of the 13½-mile Selby deviation, the first stretch of railway in the UK to be built for 125mph operation. The line opened in stages during 1983. By providing this new route BR was able to release land underneath the old East Coast main line for coal mining; it also meant that trains would no longer be slowed by the unimprovable 40mph speed restriction over Selby swing bridge. New curves at Hambleton enabled stretches of the Selby deviation to be used by York-Selby-Hull trains and by freight between Doncaster and Gascoigne Wood.

A shorter stretch of new railway opened in Rotherham in 1987 to enable local trains to call at Rotherham Central instead of the less conveniently located Masborough station. Three years later, a new connection between Swinton and Mexborough would enable Rotherham-Doncaster trains to call at the new Swinton station as well as Rotherham Central.

The Padiham branch in Lancashire enjoyed a brief revival when Padiham power station started taking trainloads of Cumbrian coal in late 1991. Because the power station had no hopper discharge facility, the trains comprised POA open wagons that had previously carried aggregates. 60032 is pictured at Padiham on 16 November 1991 after arriving with a train from Maryport. The flow lasted until March 1993 and then the coal started moving in the reverse direction, as stocks still remained on the ground when the power station closed. The branch from Rose Grove was placed out of use in December 1993. The trackbed has since been transformed into the Padiham Greenway for walkers and cyclists. (*Paul Shannon*)

The Ripley branch in Derbyshire lost its regular passenger service in 1930, but much of the branch remained open for coal from Denby until March 1999. 58004 crawls to a halt at Coxbench crossing with empty hoppers for loading at Denby on 8 July 1993. When loaded, the train would form the 1159 departure to Drakelow power station. Progress along the branch was slow because of the need for a travelling shunter to open and close the level crossing gates, although towards the end, the shunter travelled separately in a road vehicle, which speeded things up. (*Paul Shannon*)

The demise of Britain's last train ferry link between Dover and Dunkerque was not exactly a line closure but was certainly a major infrastructure change. A purpose-built vessel, the *Nord-Pas de Calais*, replaced two older ships on the route in January 1988, but the costs of the operation were still high – the cost per wagon-mile was quoted as being ten times greater than on the railway – and the ferry lost most of its traffic once the Channel Tunnel opened for business. Pilot locos 08698 and 09016 share the task of unloading the *Nord-Pas de Calais* at Dover on 17 February 1994. Loading and unloading was always carried out on both tracks simultaneously in order to maintain the correct balance. The last sailing of the train ferry took place on 22 December 1995. It is a sad fact that the Channel Tunnel today carries less rail freight than used to be carried by the train ferry. (*Paul Shannon*)

Having closed in the 1960s, the 4½-mile line from Skinningrove to Boulby reopened in April 1974 to carry potash and rock salt from a new mine at Boulby. The use of rail was stipulated in order to keep heavy lorries off the local roads. Although there were some long-distance rail movements for a time, most of the trains from Boulby ran either to Tees Dock or Middlesbrough Goods. At busy times, Boulby could produce up to eight trains a day. On 23 February 1995, 60007 *Robert Adam* crosses the 1970s bridge just east of Skinningrove with 6P23, the 1355 departure from Boulby. Today the railway is still in operation, but the trains carry polyhalite instead of potash. (*Paul Shannon*)

The building of the Channel Tunnel did not only mean the construction of a 31-mile international railway tunnel; it also required the laying of many miles of track in the Folkestone area, including the Cheriton terminal for shuttle trains and Dollands Moor sidings for rail freight. This view from the cab of a freight train on 31 May 2001 shows the exit lines from Cheriton and the English tunnel portal under Castle Hill. On the right behind the high security fencing are the tracks carrying incoming trains. Movements through the tunnel are regulated by cab signalling and the sign with the yellow triangle is a block marker indicating the start of a signalling section. (*Paul Shannon*)

The Great Central Railway between Nottingham and Leicester closed as a through route in 1969, but on the northern half of the line BR continued to serve freight customers at Hotchley Hill and Ruddington. Initially, these locations were reached from the Nottingham end, which required a run round movement in central Nottingham. In order to release the Nottingham site for redevelopment, BR restored access to Hotchley Hill and Ruddington from the south by building a new curve at Loughborough, which opened in April 1974. Both locations then stopped receiving traffic by rail, but in 2000, the British Gypsum works at Hotchley Hill started receiving trainloads of desulphogypsum. 66219 sets back at Hotchley Hill after arriving with one such train on 26 July 2001. This stretch of line is now shared by freight movements and heritage trains operated by the Great Central Railway (Nottingham). (*Paul Shannon*)

The line from Goole to Gilberdyke, providing the shortest route to Hull from the south, was proposed for closure in the 1980s because of problems with this swing bridge across the River Ouse just east of Goole. The bridge had been seriously damaged by ships in 1973 and 1976 and, rather than paying up to £2 million to repair it, BR proposed closing the route and diverting Hull trains via Selby. In the end, Humberside County Council contributed to the repair costs and the bridge has survived into the twenty-first century, benefiting from major refurbishment which included the repair and upgrading of steelwork, track renewal and the repainting. The Goole bridge and its overhead cabin dating back to 1868 are pictured from the cab of a freight train on 1 August 2005. (*Paul Shannon*)

In London, the most significant reopening of the 1980s was the Farringdon to Blackfriars link, allowing the start-up of Thameslink trains between the Midland main line and the Southern Region. A similar development in Birmingham saw the restoration of trains between Moor Street and Snow Hill. In Manchester, the new Windsor Link allowed through running between the Bolton line and Manchester Oxford Road, opening up a new route for local and long-distance trains. On the south side of the city a new connection at Hazel Grove enabled Sheffield trains to call at Stockport.

In South Wales, the Aberdare branch was the first of several former freight-only lines to rejoin the passenger network. In Scotland, the reopenings of Airdrie-Drumgelloch and Newbridge Junction-Bathgate foreshadowed the eventual return of through Edinburgh-Glasgow trains via Bathgate. Another small project that would lead to something bigger was the reopening of the Oxford-Bicester line. In Yorkshire, the Huddersfield-Sheffield service

was placed on a more secure footing once it switched from the direct Penistone-Sheffield line to the reopened Penistone-Barnsley section. One reopening that faltered was Kettering-Corby, lasting only from April 1987 until June 1990 on the first attempt.

Since 1990, the rate of passenger closures has declined to a trickle, while freight-only lines have remained vulnerable to changes in the industries that use them. Many railway openings and reopenings have taken place, ranging from busy suburban commuter routes to slick airport connections and the Channel Tunnel Rail Link (HS1).

The few genuine passenger closures of the last 30 years have included the Elmers End-Addiscombe line in Croydon and the Croxley Green branch in Hertfordshire, the latter being a sad tale of frustration as a bold scheme to reroute the Metropolitan line into Watford Junction failed to attract the necessary funding. The Stratford-North Woolwich line closed, but much of that route is

The reopening of the Robin Hood line brought passenger trains back to Mansfield, which was often quoted as the largest town without a passenger station in the UK. The line was revived in several stages: from Nottingham to Newstead in May 1993, to Mansfield Woodhouse in November 1995, and finally to Worksop in May 1998. Single car 153365 calls at Mansfield on the 1326 Nottingham-Worksop service on 1 September 2005. The station building on the northbound platform was listed for its special architectural interest in 1978 and was used as a public house until the station reopened. (*Paul Shannon*)

The three-mile Birch Coppice branch in North Warwickshire reopened in 2002 for a flow of imported Volkswagen car parts to a new distribution terminal. The branch had previously carried coal from Birch Coppice and Baddesley collieries until 1986 and 1989 respectively. The car parts were carried in vans that travelled via the Channel Tunnel and the EWS Enterprise network. 67030 ambles along the branch with 6G42, the 1123 from Birch Coppice to Bescot, on 28 July 2006. The car parts flow ceased in 2007, but in the meantime the railway had started carrying inter-modal traffic to Birch Coppice container terminal, ensuring the survival of the branch. (*Paul Shannon*)

Regular passenger trains to Maesteg via Tondu ceased in June 1970 and Maesteg forwarded its last coal in 1988. Then, following a similar pattern to the Ebbw Vale line, Maesteg regained its passenger service in October 1992. Sprinter unit 150282 arrives at Tondu with the 0800 departure from Maesteg to Cheltenham on 18 August 2009. The track of the long-closed Blaengarw branch still diverges to the right, but an untidy pile of wooden sleepers behind the train is all that remains of the sidings that once stood on the west side of the Maesteg line. The rusty track diverging bottom left is the line from Margam, used mainly for diversions. (*Paul Shannon*)

The Nuneaton avoiding line, which carried trains on the Birmingham-Leicester line over the West Coast main line, closed in February 1992. It was of limited use because it did not serve Nuneaton station. However, with all routes through Nuneaton becoming busier, it was decided to reopen the flyover and provide a new connection between the flyover and the station, providing the best of both worlds – no pathing conflict between the Birmingham-Leicester and West Coast lines and easy interchange for passengers. The work, which included a new island platform on the east side of the station, was completed in June 2004. The reopened flyover is pictured facing west on 19 April 2011. (*Paul Shannon*)

now used by the Docklands Light Railway, while the Wimbledon-West Croydon line became part of Croydon Tramlink. In Manchester, the Bury, Altrincham and Oldham/Rochdale lines all closed as heavy rail routes but are now part of the Metrolink network.

Freight line closures since 1990 have been numerous, especially where the sole user was a deep mine or a coal-fired power station. Apart from coal, the more significant freight closures in terms of route mileage, with their last main traffic in brackets, have included Heathfield (timber), Wisbech (pet food), Fen Drayton (sand), Wirksworth (limestone), Oakamoor (sand), Caldon Low (stone), Blodwell (ballast), Amlwch (chemicals), Trawswfynydd (nuclear flasks), Burn Naze (chemicals), Redmire (stone – but has since carried occasional military traffic), Eastgate (cement), Giffen (military traffic), Methil (power station and docks) and Burghead (grain).

Lines that have closed or been made redundant as through freight-only routes since 1990 have included the Leamside line from Ferryhill to Wardley, Mouldsworth-Helsby, Claydon-Bletchley and Alloa-Dunfermline. The last two are interesting for contrasting reasons; Claydon-Bletchley is expected to carry passengers again as part of East West Rail, while Alloa-Dunfermline reopened as recently as 2008 as a through route, only to find itself without regular traffic after the closure of Longannet power station in 2016.

Two freight lines that have closed and then reopened since 1990 albeit with limited success are the Portbury branch and the Donnington branch. Portbury has handled various traffic flows including coal, biomass, gypsum and motor vehicles, but by late 2018, none of these was operating. The Donnington branch was reactivated for intermodal trains, but traffic failed to build up and the terminal has been used mainly for storage and wagon repairs.

By far the majority of reopenings since 1990 have focused on passenger traffic. In London, the development of the orbital railway has seen local trains restored to the Willesden Junction-Clapham Junction line via Kensington Olympia and to the former Broad Street line south of Dalston, the latter route now forming part of the extended East London line. The expansion of Thameslink has seen a new connection opened to the East Coast main line – only a modest increase in route mileage but a significant

After the Wellington-Newport line closed to general traffic in 1968, the 2½-mile section between Wellington and Donnington was retained to give access to the British Army base at Donnington. It received deliveries via the Speedlink wagonload network until 1991, when the line was taken out of use. Part of the military site was redeveloped in 2008 as Telford International Railfreight Park, and the branch line from Wellington reopened in February 2009. Unfortunately, the terminal attracted little traffic and the sidings at Donnington have been used mainly to store redundant electric multiple units and carry out wagon repairs. 66070 arrives at Donnington with containers from Warrington on 14 July 2011 during the period when DB Schenker ran a weekly train for the Ministry of Defence. (*Paul Shannon*)

The Portishead branch closed to passengers in 1964 and to freight in 1983, the last trainload of cement having been delivered in March 1981. Almost twenty years later, much of the branch was relaid to serve a new maritime terminal at Portbury, with an eye on carrying imported coal and motor vehicles. The reopening took place in December 2001. In the following years, the branch carried trainloads of coal, biomass, gypsum and motor vehicles, as well as occasional deliveries of containers. Viewed from the walkway alongside the M5 motorway, 66737 approaches Portbury with 6V94, the 1012 Doncaster to Portbury empty biomass wagons, on 24 July 2012. In recent times, traffic has declined, with just seasonal coal trains to Fiddlers Ferry remaining. On the other hand, pressure has been mounting to relay the last three miles to Portishead and introduce a passenger service on the branch. (*Paul Shannon*)

Ironbridge 'B' power station near Buildwas kept 6½ miles of freight-only railway alive until the power station stopped generating in November 2015. Deliveries of coal were replaced by biomass during the last few years, with GB Railfreight hauling trains from Liverpool, Ellesmere Port and Portbury. 66724 climbs through Coalbrookdale with 4F68, the 0900 Ironbridge-Liverpool Bulk Terminal biomass empties, on 8 April 2014. As with so many decommissioned freight lines, Ironbridge may yet see a revived passenger service if plans to extend the Telford Steam Railway south from Lawley come to fruition. (*Paul Shannon*)

The two refineries at Coryton and Shell Haven ensured the survival of the Thames Haven branch in the late twentieth century. However, that traffic started switching to road in the 1990s because the distances were too short for rail to be viable. The last flow, bitumen from Coryton to Llandarcy, ceased at the end of 2008. Much of the Thames Haven branch was then revived to serve the new London Gateway container port. The first loaded train from the port ran in September 2013 and traffic gradually built up, with nine scheduled departures a day by summer 2018. 70008 sets out from London Gateway with 4M56, the 1257 Freightliner train to Crewe Basford Hall, on 25 July 2014. (*Paul Shannon*)

The railway land around Stratford has changed out of all recognition since the 1970s. Railway facilities including Stratford depot, London International Freight Terminal and Stratford Freightliner terminal have given way to new roads, commercial development and some green space. The North London line between Dalston and Stratford reopened to passenger traffic in 1979 and is now firmly established as a busy urban route. Unit 378221 passes Lea Junction, west of Stratford, with a westbound train on 20 August 2014. The tracks curving round to the left carry freight trains between the North London line and the Lea Valley line. (*Paul Shannon*)

The works to eliminate conflicting movements at Norton Bridge included a new railway alignment between Little Bridgeford and Yarnfield Junction on the Stoke line, as well as a spur to Heamies for the down slow towards Crewe. The new lines opened to revenue-earning services in March 2016. 66569 comes off the new down slow line at Heamies with 4M63, the 0912 Felixstowe to Ditton train, on 14 March 2017. Behind the first few wagons the original main line curves around to the left, now reduced to three tracks after the diversion of the down slow. (*Paul Shannon*)

addition to the network. And next comes the long-awaited Elizabeth Line (formerly Crossrail), connecting the Great Western main line with routes to the east of the city – a major infrastructure project by any standards.

In the West Midlands, Birmingham Snow Hill is once again a through station since the reopening of the line to Smethwick. The Walsall-Rugeley line has reopened in stages. In the East Midlands, the big project has been the restoration of passenger trains on the Robin Hood line between Nottingham and Worksop, serving Mansfield which was renowned as Britain's largest town without a railway station. While most of the Robin Hood line uses former freight-only lines – which now see little or no freight – it was necessary to rebuild the stretch between Linby and Kirkby-in-Ashfield, partly using a new alignment. The second attempt to reopen the Corby line appears to have been successful, with a few trains also running to or from the north via Melton Mowbray.

In South Wales, the Maesteg branch, Ebbw Vale branch and Barry-Bridgend line have all reopened to passengers since 1990. In northern England, the Blackburn-Clitheroe line now has a well-established regular service after a period when it saw only seasonal trains. The Askern line is used by scheduled as well as diverted trains, while the Wakefield-Knottingley line has had its local passenger service restored. The line through Brighouse which lost most of its passenger trains in 1970 has now regained regular services in four directions – to and from Sowerby Bridge, Halifax, Mirfield and Huddersfield. In Manchester, the Ordsall chord has brought greater flexibility in train routeings, enabling trains from Leeds to Manchester Airport to call at both Victoria and Piccadilly without reversing.

Scotland has seen a significant number of passenger reopenings and openings since 1990. First came the Paisley Canal line, formerly served by Kilmacolm trains, followed

For many years, coal trains on the busy route from Immingham to the Aire Valley power stations had to follow a circuitous route that involved conflicting with InterCity trains on the East Coast main line. The solution looked simple enough on the map, although it was a major engineering project and took a long time to become reality. In June 2014, Network Rail completed a flyover across the East Coast main line at Shaftholme, linking the Stainforth-Adwick line with the Shaftholme-Knottingley route. As well as eliminating conflicts, the flyover reduced the distance covered by Immingham-Drax trains by up to 14 miles. The route has also carried other trains such as those supplying spoil to a work site at Killingholme. 66014 hauls the 1532 Killingholme to Kellingley train across the flyover on 29 September 2017. (*Paul Shannon*)

Section 1 of the Channel Tunnel Rail Link, also known as High Speed 1, opened on 28 September 2003, taking around 21 minutes off the journey time between London and Paris. The engineering features on the route include this ¾-mile bridge across the River Medway, paralleling the M2 motorway bridges. The line typically carries three or four trains an hour in each direction: an hourly Eurostar to Paris; a bi-hourly Eurostar to Brussels; and a twice-hourly Javelin to East Kent. The line is available to freight at night. A Class 395 Javelin unit heads towards London on 25 January 2018. (*Paul Shannon*)

Not all planned reopenings succeed. The disused Croxley Green branch was earmarked for conversion into part of a new route linking the Metropolitan Line with Watford Junction, but the project has now been abandoned, despite gaining Government approval in 2011 and some physical clearance work having taken place in 2013. Work stopped in 2016 due to anticipated cost overruns and an unresolved dispute over funding. The photograph shows the former Watford Stadium halt on 11 February 2018. The halt had opened in 1982 but fell into disuse some time before trains on the Croxley Green branch were withdrawn in 1996. (*Paul Shannon*)

by the Cowlairs-Springburn and Rutherglen-Whifflet lines in 1993. A short extension on the former Waverley route as far as Newcraighall opened in 2002, followed by the relaying of the Larkhall branch near Hamilton three years later. Then came the reopening of Stirling-Alloa, thankfully feasible because much of the route had been kept open for freight, followed in 2010 by the Drumgelloch-Bathgate line, creating another through route between Glasgow and Edinburgh. Finally the most ambitious scheme to date has been the revival of 33 miles of the Waverley route from Newcraighall to Tweedbank – the culmination of decades of campaigning, planning and building.

Three international airports justified the building of new main line railways in the 1990s. Stansted was the first, with a 3½-mile branch from a triangular junction on the Bishops Stortford-Cambridge line opening in 1991.

The rail service has proved popular and train frequencies are limited by the single track tunnel under the runway. Manchester Airport was reached in 1993 by a new spur from the Styal line, initially facing Manchester only but later complemented by a south-facing curve for trains from Crewe. Manchester Airport has a good range of direct train services reaching as far as Middlesbrough, Newcastle and Edinburgh. Heathrow Airport had been served by London Underground since 1977 but gained its high speed link to London Paddington thanks to a new four-mile branch from the Great Western main line in 1998. The new infrastructure in this case is owned by Heathrow Airport Holdings but maintained by Network Rail. The Heathrow branch was built purely with the dedicated Paddington service in mind; in recent years new stretches of railway have been proposed to broaden the range of direct rail destinations.

Stansted Airport joined the rail network in 1991 when BR opened a 3½-mile branch from the Liverpool Street-Cambridge line. The branch includes a tunnel under the airport runway and the junction with the main line is triangular, allowing trains to run from Cambridge and beyond as well as from London. A pair of Class 379 EMUs, with unit 379014 leading, sets out from Stansted Airport station on 21 March 2018. A Class 170 diesel unit waits at the adjacent platform face. (*Paul Shannon*)

The Ordsall chord, also known as the Castlefield curve, opened in December 2017. It provides – at long last – a direct heavy rail link between Manchester Victoria and Oxford Road stations, some four decades after the Picc-Vic tunnel proposal was abandoned. The chord enables trans-Pennine trains to run through to Manchester Airport without reversing. The only problem is that congestion on the two-track bottleneck through Oxford Road and Piccadilly is exacerbated by the new flat junction at the south end of the Ordsall chord and trains into Manchester are frequently delayed as they wait for a path. The new infrastructure is pictured from a passing train on 4 May 2018. (*Paul Shannon*)

The long-awaited tram-train finally became a reality in October 2018 when the Sheffield Supertram system was extended to a new terminus at Parkgate shopping centre, sharing heavy rail tracks through Rotherham Central. Unfortunately, the project cost five times more than planned and was almost cancelled at two points during its development. Nevertheless, the concept might prove useful where the cost of a new dedicated tram line cannot be justified. Tram-train unit 399201 stands at Parkgate on a test run on 12 October 2018 while Pacer 144008 passes on a Northern Rail service to Sheffield. (*Paul Shannon*)

If Heathrow had to wait a long time for its main line rail link, then the same can be said for cross-Channel journeys since the opening of the Channel Tunnel in 1994. The first, 46-mile long, stretch of the Channel Tunnel Rail Link – now known as HS1 – finally opened in September 2003, with the ¾-mile Medway viaduct and 2-mile North Downs tunnel featuring among its engineering landmarks. The second section of HS1, covering the 24 miles from Ebbsfleet to London St Pancras, opened in November 2007. This section includes a 1½-mile tunnel under the Thames and some 12 miles of tunnelling on the approach to London. The completion of HS1 has knocked 45 minutes off the London-Paris and London-Brussels journey times and has also facilitated fast domestic trains between London and East Kent.

Casting a glance back at the 1963 Beeching Report, Britain's rail network has in many respects fared better than expected over the past four decades. While general freight traffic has become more concentrated on key arteries such as those from deep-sea ports and many lines are now completely devoid of freight, the passenger network has bounced back from the dark days of the 1960s. The list of routes that survived the Beeching threat is long and varied; it ranges from the iconic Settle-Carlisle line, which still faced the prospect of closure in 1983, to urban routes such as Romford-Upminster, Manchester-Bury and Glasgow-East Kilbride, and diverse branches such as those to Kyle of Lochalsh, Whitby, Blaenau Ffestiniog, Sudbury and Exmouth. And few people in the immediate post-Beeching era would have predicted the large number of line reopenings that have taken place since the 1970s.

For the future, we can look forward to the brand-new infrastructure of HS2 and further developments of Crossrail in London. There is no shortage of proposals for further railway reopening schemes, some of which are more likely to succeed than others. Taking an optimistic view, we may one day see trains return to Bristol-Portishead, Uckfield-Lewes, Bedford-Cambridge and even Tweedbank-Hawick-Carlisle, as well as numerous smaller schemes. Or, more pessimistically, might new technology such as driverless road vehicles stall and perhaps reverse the railway renaissance of the twenty-first century?

PRINCIPAL PASSENGER LINE CLOSURES 1970-2018		
5.1.1970	Bewdley-Hartlebury/Kidderminster	part later reopened as Severn Valley Railway
5.1.1970	Hayfield branch	
5.1.1970	Hadfield-Penistone	remained open for freight
5.1.1970	Caernarfon branch	later temporarily reopened for freight
5.1.1970	Rose Hill-Macclesfield	
5.1.1970	Cowdenbeath-Hilton Junction	
2.2.1970	Skipton-Colne	
4.5.1970	Bourne End-High Wycombe	
4.5.1970	Lowestoft-Yarmouth South Town	
1.6.1970	Fleetwood branch	part remained open for freight
22.6.1970	Bridgend-Maesteg-Cymmer Afan	
5.10.1970	Rochdale-Bolton	part remained open for freight
5.10.1970	Peterborough-Spalding-Boston	Peterborough-Spalding remained open for freight and later reopened to passengers
5.10.1970	Firsby Jn-Grimsby	Louth-Grimsby remained open for freight
5.10.1970	Willoughby-Mablethorpe	
5.10.1970	Lincoln-Firsby Jn	Lincoln-Bardney remained open for freight
5.10.1970	Ilfracombe branch	
5.10.1970	Cambridge-St Ives	part remained open for freight
2.1.1971	Minehead branch	later reopened as heritage line
3.1.1972	Swanage branch	part remained open for freight
6.3.1972	Penrith-Keswick	
6.3.1972	Birmingham Snow Hill-Wolverhampton	part remained open for freight; part later reopened to passengers
17.4.1972	Liverpool Central-Gateacre	part later reopened
5.6.1972	Crediton-Okehampton	later reopened for seasonal and heritage trains
5.6.1972	Bury-Rawtenstall	remained open for freight
28.10.1972	Paignton-Kingswear	transferred to Dart Valley Railway Company
5.2.1973	Alton-Winchester	part later reopened as Watercress Line
23.7.1973	Newcastle Riverside loop	part remained open for freight
26.8.1973	Northampton-Market Harborough	remained open for freight, excursions and diversions
22.10.1973	Kilmarnock-Dalry	
5.5.1975	Bridport branch	
1.5.1976	Alston branch	part re-laid as narrow-gauge heritage railway
3.10.1976	Gannow Jn-Hall Royd Jn (Copy Pit line)	remained open for seasonal use; later reopened all year round; freight returned June 1987
9.10.1977	Edge Hill-Bootle	remained open for freight
23.1.1978	Newcastle Central-West Monkseaton	later reopened as Tyne & Wear Metro
10.9.1979	West Monkseaton-Tynemouth	later reopened as Tyne & Wear Metro
11.8.1980	Heaton-Tynemouth	later reopened as Tyne & Wear Metro
1.6.1981	South Shields branch	later reopened as Tyne & Wear Metro
4.10.1982	Wath Road Jn-Cudworth-Normanton	remained open until 1987 for diversions and excursions; closed to all traffic 1.6.1987
29.11.1982	March-Spalding	

PRINCIPAL PASSENGER LINE CLOSURES 1970-2018		
10.1.1983	Kilmacolm branch	
10.1.1983	Paisley Canal line	part later reopened
24.1.1983	Clayton West branch	part re-laid to 15in gauge as Kirklees Light Railway
13.5.1983	Woodside-Sanderstead	later reopened as Tramlink
16.5.1983	Penistone-Sheffield	part remained open for freight
24.9.1983	Selby-York	ECML diverted
8.7.1985	Tunbridge Wells C-Eridge	part later reopened as Spa Valley Railway
8.7.1985	Tottenham Hale-Stratford	later reopened
30.6.1986	Dalston-London Broad Street	Richmond trains ceased 12.5.1985; part later reopened
17.8.1991	Manchester Victoria-Bury	later reopened as Metrolink
27.12.1991	Cornbrook Jn-Timperley	later reopened as Metrolink
25.9.1992	Camden Road-Camden Junction	remained open for freight
22.3.1996	Watford High St-Croxley Green	service suspended; offically closed 29.9.2003
2.6.1997	Wimbledon-West Croydon	later reopened as Tramlink
2.6.1997	Elmers End-Addiscombe	
9.12.2006	Stratford-North Woolwich	part later reopened as Docklands Light Railway
3.10.2009	Thorpes Bridge Jn-Oldham-Rochdale	later reopened as Metrolink

PRINCIPAL PASSENGER LINE OPENINGS AND REOPENINGS 1970-2018		
7.6.1971	Peterborough-Spalding	
5.5.1975	Barassie-Kilmarnock	
6.10.1975	Ladybank-Perth	
4.10.1976	Sinfin branch	last train ran 17.5.1993
2.5.1977	Leamington Spa-Coventry	
2.5.1977	Liverpool Moorfields-Central (link)	
9.5.1977	Liverpool James St-Lime St-Central (loop)	
3.1.1978	Liverpool Central-Garston	
14.5.1979	Dalston-Stratford	
5.11.1979	Partick-Rutherglen (Argyle line)	
16.5.1983	Penistone-Barnsley	
16.5.1983	Hambleton-Colton Jn (Selby diversion)	
16.5.1983	Garston-Hunts Cross	
30.9.1983	Temple Hirst-Hambleton (Selby diversion)	
1.10.1984	Gannow Jn-Hall Royd Jn (Copy Pit line)	previously used by seasonal services
13.5.1985	Bradford Jn-Thingley Jn	
24.3.1986	Newbridge Jn-Bathgate	
12.5.1986	Hazel Grove-New Mills South Jn	
12.4.1987	Rotherham Holmes curve	
13.4.1987	Kettering-Corby	closed 2.6.1990, later reopened again
11.5.1987	Coventry-Nuneaton	
11.5.1987	Oxford-Bicester	
5.10.1987	Birmingham Snow Hill-Moor Street	

5.10.1987	Radyr-Ninian Park-Cardiff (Cardiff City line)	
11.4.1988	Salford Crescent-Ordsall Lane (Windsor link)	initially westbound line only
16.5.1988	Farringdon-London Blackfriars	
3.10.1988	Abercynon-Aberdare	
10.4.1989	Walsall-Hednesford	
15.5.1989	Airdrie-Drumgelloch	
15.5.1989	Navigation Road-Stockport	
19.3.1990	Swinton-Mexborough	
27.7.1990	Paisley Canal branch	
19.3.1991	Stansted Airport branch	
11.5.1992	Wakefield-Knottingley	
28.9.1992	Bridgend-Maesteg	
16.5.1993	Manchester Airport branch	south-facing curve opened 15.1.1996
17.5.1993	Nottingham-Newstead	
23.8.1993	Cowlairs-Springburn	
4.10.1993	Rutherglen-Whifflet	
29.5.1994	Blackburn-Clitheroe	previously used by seasonal services
31.5.1994	Willesden Jn-Kensington Olympia	restoration of local services
24.9.1995	Birmingham Snow Hill-Smethwick	
20.11.1995	Newstead-Mansfield Woodhouse	
2.6.1997	Hednesford-Rugeley Town	extended to Rugeley Trent Valley 25.5.1998
25.5.1998	Walsall-Wolverhampton	local services withdrawn again in 2008
25.5.1998	Mansfield Woodhouse-Worksop	with 4 intermediate stations
23.6.1998	Heathrow Airport branch	
31.5.1999	Eastleigh-Romsey	
28.5.2000	Bradley Jn-Bradley Wood Jn via Brighouse	
28.5.2000	Halifax-Brighouse-Bradley Jn	
28.5.2000	Greetland Jn-Dryclough Jn	
4.6.2002	Portobello Jn-Newcraighall	
28.9.2003	Channel Tunnel-Fawkham Junction (HS1)	
12.6.2005	Barry-Bridgend	
12.12.2005	Larkhall branch	
14.11.2007	Ebbsfleet-London St Pancras (HS1)	
6.2.2008	Ebbw Jn-Ebbw Vale	
19.5.2008	Stirling-Alloa	
23.2.2009	Kettering-Corby-Manton Jn	
27.4.2010	Dalston-Hoxton	
23.5.2010	Shaftholme Jn-Knottingley via Askern	
12.12.2010	Drumgelloch-Bathgate	
6.9.2015	Newcraighall-Tweedbank	
10.12.2017	Ordsall chord	
26.2.2018	St Pancras-Belle Isle Junction (Canal Tunnels)	for Thameslink trains to Great Northern line

CHAPTER 2

STATIONS OLD AND NEW

The number of passenger stations served by Britain's rail network declined sharply in the 1960s and stabilised in the 1970s before gradually increasing from the 1980s onwards. The fall from 2,750 stations in 1967 to 2,358 stations in 1977 was largely the result of line closures proposed in the Beeching Report. However, a few stations on retained lines also closed, sometimes because they were a lightly used stopping point on an InterCity route. An example was the West Coast main line station of

Beattock, which was only served by selected Carlisle-Glasgow trains and closed in 1972 because BR could not justify the expense of updating it as part of the West Coast electrification scheme. Another example was Ashchurch, which until its closure in 1971 was the only intermediate station on the cross-country main line between Worcester and Cheltenham. However, Ashchurch station reopened in 1997, by which time the line carried more semi-fast trains that could call there.

By the early 1970s, the 10-platform terminus at Bradford Exchange had become too large for its declining usage, even though it had gained some long-distance trains at the expense of Bradford Forster Square. It was therefore replaced in January 1973 by a four-platform station about fifty yards south of the old site, also releasing land for redevelopment. The photograph shows the old station in 1970, still sporting the tangerine signs of the BR North Eastern Region. On the right is a Class 25-hauled train which, judging by its headcode, was probably the Bradford portion of a Leeds-Kings Cross express. (*Marcus Eavis/Online Transport Archive*)

Despite its convenient location for the City of London, Fenchurch Street station was being considered for possible downgrading in the late 1960s, with plans to divert its trains to Liverpool Street outside the morning and evening rush hours. Thankfully those plans were soon abandoned; today Fenchurch Street ranks as the 24th busiest station in the UK, with over 19,000 passengers using its four platforms each year. The neat frontage is pictured in 1971; it has changed little in the intervening decades except that more space is now devoted to pedestrians than cars. (*Marcus Eavis/Online Transport Archive*)

If BR had had its way, Marylebone would have been the first main-line terminus in London to face complete closure. The station lost its long-distance trains in September 1966, when the ex-Great Central main line between Calvert and Rugby was closed completely. Investment at Marylebone during the 1970s and early 1980s was minimal and semaphore signals continued to control the movements of ageing suburban DMUs. Then a serious proposal was made to convert the line from Northolt Junction to Marylebone into a reserved road for express coaches and to establish Marylebone as London's main coach station. Fortunately sense prevailed and the rails were reprieved; Marylebone is now the thriving terminus of Chiltern Railways trains from Birmingham and beyond. The elegant cast iron *porte cochère* in front of the terminus, which survives today, is pictured in 1971. (*Marcus Eavis/Online Transport Archive*)

Liverpool Exchange faced major cutbacks following the 1963 Beeching Report, which – bizarrely – proposed the closure of the busy Southport line as well as the line to Wigan via Kirkby while leaving the route to Preston via Ormskirk intact. As things turned out, it was the Preston line which suffered the most, with the withdrawal of long-distance services via Preston in 1970. This left Exchange with electric services to Southport and Ormskirk and diesel trains on the Wigan line. A visit in 1972 finds one Class 502 EMU waiting to depart and two Calder Valley Class 110 DMUs in the side platforms. Exchange station closed completely in April 1977 in readiness for the diversion of its electric trains via Moorfields. (*Marcus Eavis/Online Transport Archive*)

The frontage of the doomed Liverpool Exchange station is pictured in 1975, by which time work on the Northern Line tunnel via Moorfields would have been well advanced. After closure in 1977, the platform area of Exchange became a car park, while the station frontage was retained and later incorporated into the Mercury Court office complex. (*Harry Luff/Online Transport Archive*)

The nineteenth century railway builders left Liverpool with three separate termini and, when train services were rationalised in the post-Beeching era, it made sense to improve connectivity by channelling as much traffic as possible through a single location. Liverpool Central High Level closed in April 1972, a casualty of the major reshaping of Liverpool's network which would eventually see all long-distance and diesel-worked suburban trains concentrated on Lime Street and electric trains using two interconnected tunnels – the north-south link line for Southport, Ormskirk, Kirkby and Garston and the loop line for the Wirral. The frontage of Central is pictured in 1975 when the High Level platforms were already closed but the Low Level station was still a terminating line from the Wirral. (*Harry Luff/Online Transport Archive*)

Sudbury's second station, opened in 1865, lay on the through line from Marks Tey to Shelford via Haverhill. The Sudbury-Shelford section closed to all traffic in 1967 and the Marks Tey-Sudbury stretch very nearly closed as well but was reprieved in 1974 thanks to a subsidy agreed by Essex and Suffolk county councils. Sudbury station became unstaffed in 1966 and for a time the buildings lay derelict, as seen in this photograph from 1972. After a period of inevitable decay, the station closed in October 1991 and was replaced by a new, more compact facility a short distance to the east. (*Harry Luff/Online Transport Archive*)

Southminster station still had the feel of a country branch terminus when this Class 104 DMU was photographed waiting to depart for Wickford in 1973. The station had lost its general goods facilities in 1965 but the run round loop was retained for nuclear flasks from Bradwell power station, which were loaded in a compound just outside the station. It was undoubtedly the nuclear traffic which helped to assure the line's future. The scene at Southminster would change dramatically by 1986 when overhead electrification was energised, removing one of the last pockets of diesel operation in Essex. (*Harry Luff/Online Transport Archive*)

Some city centre stations outlived the withdrawal of passengers as parcels terminals. A good example was Nottingham London Road Low Level, which closed to passengers in 1944 but survived for parcels traffic until 1988. Parcels vans do little to enhance the French château style station building with its Romanesque *porte cochère* in this photograph from 1977. Parcels traffic declined sharply throughout BR in the 1980s and it was no surprise when London Road was declared surplus to requirements. (*Marcus Eavis/Online Transport Archive*)

Manors station, located just half a mile from Newcastle Central, was once a busy suburban hub with no less than nine platforms, serving the various lines to the coast as well as local trains on the East Coast main line. A Class 104 DMU calls at Manors in 1977. The conversion of the North Tyneside loop to Metro operation deprived Manors of much of its traffic from 1978 onwards. Today, all that remains of the once sprawling facility is a single island platform, served by hourly stopping trains between Newcastle and Morpeth. (*Harry Luff/Online Transport Archive*)

Matlock Bath was one of the first station reopenings of the post-Beeching era. It had closed in March 1967 when local passenger services between Derby and Chinley were withdrawn. It reopened as an unstaffed halt in May 1972. The station building was listed in 1971, the 'Swiss chalet' style having been inspired by comparisons with Alpine scenery when it was built in the mid-nineteenth century. In recent years, the station has been adopted by Matlock Bath parish council who have spruced it up for the benefit of visiting and resident passengers. On 14 April 1977, a Class 120 DMU calls with a Matlock-Derby service. (*Paul Shannon*)

Opened in May 1972, Bristol Parkway was the first of a new generation of Parkway stations, located on green field sites to cater for people arriving and departing by car. Its position enabled it to act as an interchange point between trains on the South Wales main line and those on the cross-country Birmingham-Bristol route. An InterCity 125 train calls at Bristol Parkway on 10 September 1977. Passenger numbers grew rapidly and in recent decades the number of platforms has been increased from two to four. A new station building with an enclosed footbridge and lifts was commissioned in 2001. (*Paul Shannon*)

In addition to its through lines, Manchester Victoria once had ten bay platforms on the south side, catering for local trains to Bury, Oldham, Rochdale and other destinations to the north east of the city. Four of those platforms were taken out of use in 1973 because the land was required for the proposed Picc-Vic tunnel, a project that was later cancelled because of the cost. A Class 504 EMU comprising cars M77173 and M65452 leaves one of the surviving bay platforms with a service for Bury on 25 July 1979. The number of bay platforms has since been reduced to just two, making space for the Metrolink tracks which took over the Bury service in 1992. (*Paul Shannon*)

A trend which helped to save stations on retained lines from possible closure was the shutting of booking offices and withdrawal of station staff. From the late 1960s, many lightly used lines switched to Paytrain operation, with some or all of their stations becoming unstaffed halts. In North West England, for example, Leeds-Hellifield-Morecambe became a Paytrain route in 1970 and the Preston-Colne and Preston-Ormskirk lines in 1971. Between 1967 and 1979, the number of unstaffed stations on BR increased from 365 to 645.

As well as helping to save stations – and lines – from closure, Paytrain operation sometimes led to a restored service on Sundays where calls had previously only been possible during the weekday opening hours of the booking office. For example, in the 1972 timetable, a Sunday service became possible at a number of intermediate stations between Carnforth and Barrow, and at Blythe Bridge and Longton on the Stoke-Derby line. Paytrain operation would also encourage the provision of new or reopened stations by keeping their running costs down. A very early example of this was Garston station on the St Albans Abbey branch, which opened in 1966 as an unstaffed halt at the same time as other stations on the line lost their staff.

The Paytrain trend continued into the 1980s. Staff were withdrawn in 1985 from twelve stations across West and South Yorkshire, including Wakefield Kirkgate, and in 1988 from five intermediate stations between Wolverhampton and Shrewsbury. The obvious limitation with Paytrain operation was the challenge of collecting fares during busy periods, or where trains were formed of more than two or more units with no corridor connection between them.

Even where station staff were retained, BR could reduce costs by removing ticket barriers and carrying out ticket checks on the train. The Open Station System was widely adopted during the 1980s. On the Western Region, for example, BR had withdrawn routine ticket checks from all stations west of Highbridge (now Highbridge and Burnham) by early 1982 and from a much wider area including Newport, Bristol, Bath, Newbury, Swindon and Oxford by the end of 1985. The policy gave some stations a more welcoming feel and eliminated possible congestion at the ticket barrier. On the other hand, ticketless travel became an increasing problem because on-train checks were not always reliable. In recent years, many stations have had electronic ticket gates installed in a reversal of the 1980s policy.

Returning to individual station closures, a few lightly used rural halts disappeared from the network because, even though they were already unstaffed, the costs of maintaining them or upgrading them to modern safety standards were prohibitive. On the Cambrian Coast line, trains stopped calling at the remote Black Rock Halt in 1976 and at Abertafol and Gogarth in 1984. These three halts might well have been targeted sooner, but it made sense to retain them while the whole line was under threat of closure. A further casualty on the Cambrian Coast was Llangelynin in 1991, this tiny halt being judged unsafe because it had no lighting.

In Scotland, Errol station between Perth and Dundee closed in 1985, only one objection having been received to the closure proposal; however, its neighbour Invergowrie survived thanks to a subsidy from Tayside Regional Council. In Yorkshire, the tiny halt at Altofts closed in 1990, allowing trains between Leeds and Wakefield Kirkgate to be diverted via Castleford. In Dorset, no trains called at Radipole Halt near Weymouth after December 1983 because of concerns about the safety of the wooden platforms, and its official closure took place in the following year.

Station closures have not been limited to rural areas. In a few cases the run-down of industry meant that stations outlived their usefulness. On Teesside, industry gradually moved away from the corridor alongside the railway, resulting in the closure of Cargo Fleet and Grangetown stations in 1990 and 1991 respectively. On the same line, South Bank station had been re-sited in 1984 to make way for redevelopment, while Warrenby Halt had been replaced by British Steel Redcar to allow the railway to be diverted around the expanding steelworks. In Sheffield, both Attercliffe Road and Brightside stations closed in 1995 following the decline of local industry; in the latter case, passengers could switch to the nearby Meadowhall station which opened in 1990.

A number of stations across the network have been relocated either to meet changed needs or to release land for redevelopment – and sometimes for both reasons together. In 1973, the sprawling and under-utilised ten-platform terminus at Bradford Exchange was closed in favour of today's more practical four-platform station, since renamed Bradford Interchange. A large area of prime city centre land was sold off, while the new station – albeit slightly further away from the city centre – enjoyed better interchange facilities with buses. In 1990,

The track layout at Britain's most northerly station, Thurso, had changed little since the nineteenth century when photographed on 24 September 1980. The passenger terminus still boasted a run round loop because all trains were locomotive hauled, in this instance by 26042. Two mineral wagons wait to discharge their coal on the left, while the goods yard on the right remains intact, even with a van in the goods shed – which was a real rarity by this time. In the background are a crane and a trailer, indicating that BR still operated a lifting and delivery service for goods at Thurso. (*Paul Shannon*)

A far cry from the busy nine-platform terminus of the early twentieth century, London Broad Street had declined by the 1980s to a crumbling, half-deserted shell, with only two platforms in regular use. The station had never been fully repaired after sustaining bomb damage in the Second World War and the overall roof was shortened in 1967/68. A Class 501 unit waits to depart for Richmond on 27 February 1981. The only services remaining after May 1985 were peak hour trains to Watford Junction; demolition contractors moved in soon after that and the trains used a temporary platform at the north end of the station until they ceased altogether in June 1986. (*Paul Shannon*)

Typical of the low cost but effective stations that BR built in the 1970s and 1980s was Ruskington, serving a rural community on the Sleaford-Lincoln line. It opened in 1975 to replace the original station that had closed in 1961. A four-car DMU formation with a Class 105 set leading calls at Ruskington on 20 June 1981. In recent years, the station has been upgraded and step free access is now possible to both platforms without using the barrow crossing. The signal box closed in May 1982. (*Paul Shannon*)

Bedford St Johns had been a through station on the Oxford to Cambridge line until that route closed in January 1968. St Johns then became the terminus for the local service from Bletchley, but that too was threatened by closure in 1972. In the meantime, St Johns had become unstaffed and lost its buildings apart from a small remnant of the train shed supported on girders. The forlorn platform is pictured on 28 July 1981, with Class 105 cars M50390 and M56482 waiting to return to Bletchley. The station closed in May 1984, when the trains were diverted to the Midland station in Bedford. A small replacement halt for St Johns was provided on the curve bypassing the old station. (*Paul Shannon*)

Many BR stations remained partly gas lit long after electricity became the norm. Ilkley was the last station on the network to retain working gas lamps on the platform. They were extinguished for the last time on 8 May 1988. A Class 101 DMU is pictured at Ilkley on 17 December 1981. At that time, the station still boasted four platforms – a reminder of the time when through trains ran to Skipton – but they would be reduced to two in 1983. Today the station has electric trains as well as electric lighting. (*Paul Shannon*)

Cargo Fleet was one of several small stations between Middlesbrough and Redcar which served the ribbon of heavy industry along the south bank of the Tees estuary. As industrial activity declined, so did the stations. Cargo Fleet became an unstaffed halt in 1969 and the station buildings were soon demolished, leaving just a small shelter for waiting passengers. A Class 101 DMU calls with a train for Saltburn on 20 March 1982. Faced with the need for costly repairs, BR proposed closing Cargo Fleet and, with very few objections, the closure went ahead in January 1990. The platform was later removed to allow the westbound track to be realigned. (*Paul Shannon*)

Tilbury Riverside is a rare example of a passenger station which became a freight terminal in the late twentieth century. Originally built to connect with boats across and along the Thames, Tilbury Riverside lost much of its business after the opening of the Dartford Tunnel in 1963. Class 302 EMU 270 waits at the station on 18 April 1984. Tilbury Riverside continued to operate with declining passenger numbers and closed in November 1992. The site was then converted into a rail-served freight terminal, which remained active until 2019. The flows handled include tinplate from Trostre and intermodal traffic from Barry. (*Paul Shannon*)

Built on the site of Alfreton station which had closed in 1967, Alfreton & Mansfield Parkway opened in May 1973. It was designed as a stopping place for InterCity trains and, as its name suggested, it aspired to serve the town of Mansfield which had been station-less since 1964. For a time, Alfreton & Mansfield Parkway did what it was designed to do, offering useful free parking as well as good long-distance train services. However, it gradually focused more on local traffic and parking charges were eventually introduced. The opening of Mansfield station on the Robin Hood line in 1995 prompted a reversion to the pre-1964 name of Alfreton. The station is pictured in its InterCity days with 47433 hauling the 1009 Barrow-in-Furness to Nottingham train on 24 July 1984. (*Paul Shannon*)

Bradford Forster Square was once busy with long-distance and local passenger trains and with particularly heavy parcels traffic, but by the early 1980s it handled only local trains to Ilkley and Keighley. On 29 September 1984, a Class 108 DMU is dwarfed by its semi-derelict surroundings as it rolls into Forster Square on an Ilkley service. Further rationalisation was not far away: Most of the station site was sold for redevelopment and in June 1990, a replacement three-platform station was provided on the western fringe. Train services gradually improved, with electrification in 1994 and the restoration of both InterCity services and local trains to Leeds via Shipley. (*Paul Shannon*)

While many stations lost their nineteenth century ironwork, Hellifield was one of the more fortunate locations where Midland Railway logos and other ornate features survived long enough to become listed structures in the 1970s. A Class 110 DMU calls with a Morecambe train on 2 June 1985. Having lost its railway staff in 1975, Hellifield suffered from neglect and its buildings faced the prospect of demolition despite their listed status. Fortunately, a cash injection was provided by BR in conjunction with English Heritage and the Railway Heritage Trust. Today the buildings house a pleasant privately-run café and the ironwork has been smartly repainted. (*Paul Shannon*)

Bradford's other railway terminus, Forster Square, was likewise pruned, with a compact three-platform station located on the western edge of the former railway land. For many years, Forster Square had been busy with parcels as well as passenger traffic, but this had all but disappeared by the early 1980s.

Further examples of station relocation to release land were Morecambe, which moved a short distance back from the seafront in 1994, and Wrexham Central, which migrated 300 yards to the west in 1996. In Scotland, Fort William station was relocated half a mile out of town in 1975 to make way for a new road.

On the East Coast main line, Stevenage station was relocated nearer to the modern town centre in 1973, and the new station took over from Hitchin as an InterCity stopping point. In Liverpool, the former main-line termini at Central and Exchange closed in 1975 and 1977 respectively, to be replaced by the underground stations at Moorfields and Central Low Level. Both the original

termini had handled only local traffic in their last few years, with long-distance trains diverted to Liverpool Lime Street. Two small stations which moved mainly for passengers' convenience were Upton-by-Chester, replaced by Bache in 1984, and Filton, replaced by Filton Abbey Wood in 1996.

At Gloucester, the closure of Eastgate station in 1975 eliminated four city-centre level crossings and concentrated all traffic on Gloucester Central, although trains to and from Bristol were now faced with a time-consuming reversal. There were some parallels with Gloucester at Lincoln, where the closure of St Marks coupled with the building of a new curve allowed all trains to use Lincoln Central from May 1985, although in this instance one troublesome level crossing was replaced by the shared use of another.

Several stations have been relocated because of changes in the local railway network. At Bedford, the former St Johns station on the Cambridge line was

Although the new town of Telford was developed in the 1960s, it took two decades for a new station to be built to serve it. The nearest existing stations were Oakengates and Wellington, together with New Hadley halt which closed in 1985. Telford Central was built with InterCity trains in mind and enjoyed easy access from the M54 motorway as well as from the surrounding housing estates. It opened in May 1986. The construction phase is pictured on 21 August 1985 as a Class 108 DMU passes through on its way to Shrewsbury. (*Paul Shannon*)

Smithy Bridge station, north of Rochdale, closed in 1960 but reopened with a slightly different platform layout on 19 August 1985. This view from the crossing box shows a DMU comprising Class 110 and Class 108 vehicles calling with an eastbound train on 25 January 1986. The box closed in 2014 when the level crossing came under the supervision of Castleton. (*Paul Shannon*)

Bury Interchange was opened by BR in March 1980 to replace the old Bury Bolton Street station on the Manchester-Rawtenstall line. The new station was built as a terminus as BR had no intention of resuming through passenger trains to Rawtenstall, even though at that time the line to Rawtenstall was still open for freight. Two Class 504 EMUs stand at Bury Interchange on 23 February 1986, with the unique side contact third rail visible in the foreground. Heavy rail gave way to light rail when the Bury line became part of the Metrolink network in April 1992. (*Paul Shannon*)

Serving a sparsely populated area, Altofts station on the Leeds-Normanton line did well to survive its listing in the 1963 Beeching Report. A relatively busy moment is captured on 14 July 1986 as Class 101 cars E51433 and E51502 call on a Leeds to Sheffield service. During that year, BR proposed to close both Woodlesford and Altofts stations and divert trains via Wakefield Westgate; however, in the end, Woodlesford survived and the train service was diverted via Castleford instead. Altofts saw its last station call on 12 May 1990 and for a time the line through the station site was not used by any passenger trains. Today, trains once again pass through, but no trace of Altofts station remains. (*Paul Shannon*)

Hall i' th' Wood station on the Bolton-Blackburn line was opened by BR in September 1986 to serve a residential district with good commuting potential to Manchester. Its wooden platforms were staggered because of the limited availability of land. Class 101 cars M53318 and M53328 call at Hall i' th' Wood with a train from Blackburn on 8 November 1986. (*Paul Shannon*)

Kensington Olympia has seen several changes in its use. In the 1970s, it hosted three distinct operations: a peak-hour BR shuttle to and from Clapham Junction; London Underground shuttles to and from Earls Court when an exhibition was on at Olympia; and Motorail trains to Scotland, South Wales and South West England. The Motorail facility was closed in 1981, but new passenger services appeared in 1986 when Olympia became a calling point for InterCity trains avoiding central London. At the same time, the London Underground trains became daily. 47645 calls with a northbound InterCity working on 7 July 1987, overtaking a train of empty aggregate hoppers held on the through line. Further changes saw the gradual withdrawal of InterCity trains and the reversion of London Underground trains to exhibition periods only, but on the positive side, Olympia became a stopping point on the regular Willesden Junction-Clapham Junction service in 1994. (*Paul Shannon*)

Llanfairpwll station has been known by several other names including Llanfair, Llanfair P.G. and the long version visible in this photograph which was invented by the Victorians to attract tourists. The station was closed in 1966, reopened temporarily as a bus-rail interchange point from 1970 until 1972 while the Holyhead line was blocked due to the Britannia Bridge fire, then reopened permanently in May 1973. With plenty of evidence of tourism in the background, Sprinter unit 150128 calls with an eastbound train on 11 August 1987. (*Paul Shannon*)

Honeybourne station closed in 1969 when BR withdrew the Evesham-Stratford service and closed the Honeybourne-Stratford stretch to passengers. Further rationalisation saw the singling of the main line through Honeybourne in 1971. Since then, two of the cutbacks have been reversed. The station reopened with a single platform in May 1981 and the line was doubled again in 2011 with a second platform provided. Unit 155332 calls at Honeybourne with the 1416 Hereford-Oxford train on 29 August 1988. (*Paul Shannon*)

Manchester Victoria changed out of all recognition during the 1990s. Many of the old buildings were swept away and the number of through tracks was reduced to four to make space for the Manchester Arena. Pacer 142046 departs from the west end of the station with the 1113 Rochdale to Bolton train on 16 July 1994. In more recent times, traffic levels have recovered at Victoria, particularly since the Ordsall chord was opened and North TransPennine expresses were rerouted via the station in 2018. (*Paul Shannon*)

The twin train shed that had covered Blackburn station since the nineteenth century was replaced by a modern structure in 2000, although the original Grade II listed station frontage was retained. The interior of the rebuilt station is pictured on 29 March 2003. The refurbishment included the reinstatement of a fourth platform which had been taken out of use when the area was resignalled in 1973. (*Paul Shannon*)

Clitheroe station was removed from the BR passenger map in 1962, but the line through the town remained in use for passenger diversions as well as freight. 'Dalesrail' excursions began using the line in 1978 and Clitheroe station regained regular Summer Saturday trains in 1990. A full Blackburn-Clitheroe service resumed in May 1994. Unit 150149 is about to depart for Manchester on 29 March 2003, with the original station building – now housing an art gallery – visible on the right. (*Paul Shannon*)

The new terminus at Sudbury, built to replace the former through station pictured on page 57, opened in October 1991 on the site of the former horse dock. Unit 150245 has just arrived with the 0944 service from Marks Tey on 15 April 2003. Despite its modest appearance, the station is well cared for and has won an award in the annual 'Anglia in Bloom' competition on several occasions. (*Paul Shannon*)

replaced by a platform on the curve to Bedford Midland once trains from Bletchley were diverted to terminate at the Midland station in 1984. On the south bank of the Humber, New Holland Town and Pier stations became redundant after the ferry ceased operation and were replaced by a platform on the curve to Barton-on-Humber in June 1981. In the City of London, Holborn Viaduct was replaced by City Thameslink on the reopened route from Farringdon to Blackfriars in 1990.

A few stations have moved because their role changed. In the Manchester area, the location of Godley Junction only made sense while the branch to Stockport via Woodley was active; its 1986 replacement less than half a mile away was much closer to habitation. It was a similar situation on the Oldham loop line, where Royton Junction had long since ceased to be a junction for Royton and was replaced in 1985 by the more conveniently situated Derker. At Blaenau Ffestiniog, the Conwy Valley service was extended to a new station on the former GWR site in 1982 to join the newly restored Ffestiniog Railway. New interchange opportunities brought about the replacement of Smethwick West by Smethwick Galton Bridge in 1996 and the closure of Allerton in favour of Liverpool South Parkway in 2005/06.

Compared with the closures and relocations, a bigger trend since the late 1970s has been the opening and reopening of passenger stations. The total number of stations on the national network rose from 2,358 in 1977 to 2,405 in 1986/87, 2,498 in 1996/97, 2,522 in 2006/07 and 2,560 in 2016/17. Even those figures do not tell the whole story, because those stations that have switched to light rail operation such as Manchester Metrolink, Croydon Tramlink and Tyne and Wear Metro no longer count as part of the national network and bring the total down.

New and reopened stations fall into several categories. One is the Parkway type, located on an out of town site and designed specifically with the motorist in mind. The first example of this type – although it has never carried the Parkway name – was New Pudsey, opened in 1967 on a spacious site that was convenient for the Leeds ring road and the eastern side of Bradford. In fact, New Pudsey never quite lived up to expectations; it lost its direct London trains in 1988 and today it is a commuter station like many others. However, the Parkway idea was born.

The first station to bear the Parkway name was Bristol Parkway, opened in 1972. In contrast to New Pudsey, it was an instant success and has continued to thrive up to the present day. Located at the intersection of London-Cardiff and Birmingham-Bristol railway routes, Bristol Parkway is a popular place to change trains and it is also easily accessible by road, with the M4, M32 and M5 motorways all passing nearby. There is a fairly large local population, who use the station for short as well as long-distance journeys.

Not long after Bristol Parkway came Alfreton and Mansfield Parkway, opened in 1973 on the site of the original Alfreton station. Its aspiration to draw motorists from Mansfield, about nine miles away, was never fully satisfied and, when Mansfield gained its own station in 1995, Alfreton and Mansfield Parkway became plain Alfreton. It is, nevertheless, a fairly well used station. Another out of town station – but without the Parkway branding – opened at Birmingham International in 1976, serving the nearby airport and exhibition centre as well as taking custom from the surrounding towns and villages.

Since 1980, the national network has gained 15 new stations with the Parkway name. In addition, five existing stations have had the Parkway suffix added, although in some cases such as Didcot and Port Talbot they are not in keeping with the out of town concept. Some of the new-build Parkway stations are designed for commuter traffic, such as Horwich Parkway on the Preston-Manchester line, Aylesbury Vale Parkway on an extension of the Aylesbury-Marylebone line, and Ebbw Vale Parkway on the reopened line to Cardiff. Others target InterCity and other long-distance journeys, such as East Midlands Parkway on the Midland main line and Warwick Parkway on the Marylebone-Birmingham line.

Not all Parkway proposals have come to fruition. In 1984, the Western Region of BR was planning new Parkway stations at Hinksey for the south side of Oxford, at Barnwood for Gloucester and Cheltenham, and at Iver for the M25 on the west side of London. Those proposals were all abandoned, although Oxford now has its own Parkway station on the north side of the city near Water Eaton.

Several new stations owe their existence to airports. Alongside Manchester, Stansted and Heathrow which are each served by their dedicated branch line,

The grade II listed station at Grange-over-Sands oozes with nostalgia as it shows off the work of architect Edward Paley, who also designed many non-railway buildings in North Lancashire and present-day Cumbria. The station is also a functional one, with a ticket office, waiting rooms and step free access to both platforms. The eastbound platform is pictured on 11 July 2003. (*Paul Shannon*)

These plaques record the origins of Grange-over-Sands station and acknowledge the contributions of various bodies towards its refurbishment in 1997/98. (*Paul Shannon*)

Situated between Brookmans Park and Hatfield on the Great Northern main line, Welham Green station opened in September 1986. The grouping of tracks by direction, with the two slow lines on the outside, meant that Welham Green only needed two platforms and the track did not have to be slewed. The funding for the station came partly from Hertfordshire County Council and two local councils. Unit 313027 calls with an evening train from Welwyn Garden City to Moorgate on 21 April 2003. (*Paul Shannon*)

For 166 years, Cambridge station had to make do with several dead-end bays and a single through platform, which was long enough to hold two trains but made day-to-day operation difficult because up and down trains could not cross each other without conflicting. A new island platform was finally opened in late 2011 on the site of some redundant freight sidings, dramatically easing the pressure on timetabling and improving the railway's resilience in case of disruption. Unit 365509 stands at the new platform with a King's Cross service on 21 December 2011, while another Class 365 unit waits to head north from the original long platform. In the foreground is the diamond crossing which allowed trains to use either half of the long platform. (*Paul Shannon*)

Built more for the comfort of the Earl of Yarborough than for the convenience of villagers, Brocklesby station was situated much closer to Ulceby than to Brocklesby. The Earl, who was chairman of the Manchester Sheffield and Lincolnshire Railway when the line was built, had his own waiting room here. The station building was listed in 1985, with the unusual platform-mounted signal box gaining similar recognition ten years later. Passenger numbers at Brocklesby were never great and the station closed in October 1993. A visit on 22 August 2012 finds 66090 passing the derelict platforms with an Immingham-Cottam coal train. The box became redundant when the area was resignalled in 2015. (*Paul Shannon*)

Blackfriars station underwent major rebuilding in 2009-12, with twelve-coach platforms straddling the River Thames and a new south bank entrance. This view, dated 14 July 2017, shows the abutments that once supported a bridge carrying the westernmost tracks; that bridge was taken out of use in the early 1970s and removed in 1985. A third line of disused piers was clad in stone to support the reconstructed bridge. The platforms are covered with 4,400 photovoltaic panels which provide up to half of the energy consumed by the station. (*Paul Shannon*)

The 120ft twin brick towers and side walls are all that remain today of the original Cannon Street station, completed in 1866. The towers were grade II listed in 1972 and restored in 1986, with the weather vanes gilded to complement the dome of St Paul's Cathedral. The station sits on some of the most expensive land in the country and successive developments have sought to make the best use of the air space above the platforms. The most recent work was carried out in the late 2000s and comprised a combination of offices and retail units. The result is pictured here on 14 July 2017. For decades, Cannon Street was very much a City commuter station with no evening or Sunday trains, but that changed in 2015 when Southeastern introduced a more comprehensive timetable. (*Paul Shannon*)

The classical façade of Huddersfield station is undoubtedly one the finest in the country, meriting not only a grade I listing but also accolades from the writer and broadcaster Sir John Betjeman and the architectural scholar and writer Sir Nikolaus Pevsner. The station was completed in the 1840s, proudly overlooking St George's Square. Since 2009, the square has been a pleasant pedestrian zone, showing to good effect the statue of former Prime Minister Harold Wilson – arguably Huddersfield's most famous son – which was erected in 1999. The photograph is dated 17 July 2017. (*Paul Shannon*)

new stations on existing lines have opened at Prestwick International Airport in 1994, Luton Airport in 1999 and Southend Airport in 2011. The first and last of these stations are well situated for flyers, but the station for Luton Airport lies some distance from the air terminal, as indeed its full name Luton Airport Parkway suggests.

The most numerous new and reopened stations are those catering mainly for commuter and other local journeys. Wherever an area of housing or employment has grown up near an existing railway, then there is the chance of a new station being built but various conditions first have to be met. Every project needs a sound business case and appropriate funding. There must be good physical access and, where appropriate, space for

a car park. Any negative effects on the local community need to be taken into account: For example, not everyone wants a busy station at the bottom of their garden. And, for new stations on existing lines, there needs to be a suitable train service in place that will not be adversely affected by an additional calling point.

One of the first post-Beeching station reopenings was Narborough on the Leicester-Nuneaton line. Its service resumed in January 1970, less than two years after its closure. The cost of reopening Narborough was £3,250, which allowing for inflation equates to around £50,000 in 2018. By contrast, a typical new station today usually costs between £2 million and £12 million. Of course, Narborough was reopened rather than new, but even

Birmingham Moor Street was set to be downgraded and possibly closed in 1969 when BR announced its plans to axe the North Warwickshire line to Stratford-upon-Avon and divert most trains from the Solihull line into New Street. However, the North Warwickshire line was reprieved and from the mid-1970s Moor Street began to attract more trains – and passengers. Moor Street gained through platforms for the first time in 1987 when the tunnel to Birmingham Snow Hill was reopened. From 2002 onwards, a programme of major refurbishment gradually restored Moor Street to 1930s style, complete with reproduction lamps and station furniture. The entrance concourse is pictured on 7 February 2018. (*Paul Shannon*)

Stone station has had something of a chequered history in recent decades. It lost its rail services in 2004 while the line through Stoke-on-Trent was being upgraded, and the closure continued after the upgrading was complete because the local trains that had served it no longer ran. However, the platforms returned to use in December 2008 when London Midland introduced a semi-fast service between London Euston and Crewe via Stoke-on-Trent. The other intermediate stations on the Stafford-Stoke line were less fortunate: Norton Bridge officially closed in December 2017, while Wedgwood and Barlaston are still served by rail replacement buses at the time of writing. The listed frontage of Stone station is pictured on 12 February 2018. (*Paul Shannon*)

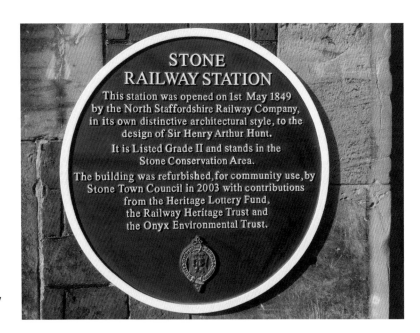

The work of the celebrated nineteenth century surveyor Sir Henry Arthur Hunt has been preserved for another generation thanks to the work coordinated by Stone Town Council in 2003. (*Paul Shannon*)

When completed in 1868, St Pancras station boasted the largest single-spanned roof in the world. Together with the adjoining Midland Grand Hotel in striking Gothic style, the station was a bold statement by the Midland Railway as it began to assert itself as one of the country's big railway companies. A century later, the future of St Pancras was far from assured – plans were mooted to combine King's Cross, St Pancras and Euston into a single huge station – but in the 1990s it could look forward to a new era as the Government opted for St Pancras as the London terminal for high-speed Channel Tunnel trains. For this purpose, the station had to be doubled in length and six platforms were added. On 7 March 2018, a line-up of Eurostar trains is dwarfed by its magnificent surroundings. (*Paul Shannon*)

This larger than life statue of Sir John Betjeman, completed in 2007, recalls the poet's foreboding words that St Pancras was 'too beautiful and too romantic to survive in a world of tower blocks and concrete'. Thankfully history proved him wrong. (*Paul Shannon*)

Completed in 1851-52 to a design by the architect Lewis Cubitt, the grade I listed façade of King's Cross station was partly hidden from view by a 1970s passenger concourse and ticket office until a major rebuilding scheme got under way in the twenty-first century. The offending buildings were removed to make way for a 75,000sqft open space, as seen here on 7 March 2018. Behind the façade, the train shed has been reglazed and decluttered, and passenger facilities have been improved with a new concourse on the western side. The project won a much-coveted European Heritage award in 2013. (*Paul Shannon*)

Built in the shadow of Ratcliffe power station, East Midlands Parkway opened in January 2009. It was intended partly as a railhead for East Midlands Airport, although in reality the four-mile distance between the station and the airport is a disincentive for many flyers. Some commuters may have been put off by high car parking charges. Overall passenger numbers at the station have been well below expectations but have shown a slight year-on-year increase since 2015. Meridian unit 222004 calls at East Midlands Parkway with a train for London St Pancras on 2 May 2018. (*Paul Shannon*)

The original Corby station closed to passengers in 1966, but the line remained open for freight and diversions. BR restored an experimental service between Kettering and a single platform on the down side in April 1987, but that service ceased in May 1990. A more permanent – and more impressive – facility was opened in February 2009, this time using a platform on the up side of the line. The hourly service to and from St Pancras, with occasional trains continuing via Oakham, has attracted a good level of custom. The Sundew sculpture, designed to reflect the steel-making heritage of Corby by depicting the change of state from liquid metal into solid form, greets travellers arriving at the station on 16 July 2018. (*Paul Shannon*)

the reopening of Lea Bridge station near Stratford in 2016 incurred a cost of more than £11 million. What has changed is partly a greater emphasis on safety and security; for example, it is no longer acceptable for passengers to use a foot crossing and any new footbridges have to be ramped or accompanied by lifts to comply with disability legislation. Some would also argue that costs are higher today because BR has been replaced by a large number of private companies, all of which need to make money.

Other early reopenings included Feniton and Needham Market in 1971, Matlock Bath and Shotton Low Level in 1972, Alness, Baildon and Llanfairpwll in 1973, and Magdalen Road, Metheringham and Ruskington in 1975. These stations were all unstaffed and their facilities

were modest. A few new stations were belatedly provided for towns that had grown up alongside railway lines after the Second World War. The 1950s town of Basildon gained its own station in 1974, and in Greater Manchester the 1960s overspill estates of Brinnington and Hattersley acquired stations in 1977 and 1978 respectively.

Gradually the rate of station openings and reopenings gathered pace. During the 1980s, well over 100 stations were added to the BR network, many on previously used sites but some entirely new. South and West Yorkshire proved to be particularly fertile ground for reopenings. Between 1982 and 1984 seven new or reopened stations appeared on the map, to be joined by several more by the end of the decade. 1986 saw the return of scheduled stopping trains on the Settle to Carlisle line, bringing eight intermediate stations back to life. Milton Keynes finally gained its own InterCity station in 1982, while in Shropshire, Telford Central opened in 1986. At the other end of the scale, the tiny Sugar Loaf Halt on the Central Wales line reopened in 1984, its annual passenger footfall rarely exceeding 200.

Since 1990, further schemes have brought the total number of stations opened or reopened since the Beeching era to around 370. South and West Yorkshire have featured prominently in the list, but most parts of the network have seen some growth. In Scotland, more than 45 stations opened or reopened between 1990 and 2017. Most of those stations formed additional stopping points on existing lines, stretching from Gretna Green on the English border to Beauly and Conon Bridge on the Far North and Kyle of Lochalsh lines. South Wales has also fared well, with more than 20 station openings or reopenings since 1990.

Given the many hurdles that new and reopened station projects face, it is remarkable that so many towns and villages have had their rail service restored in the past four decades. The point is well illustrated by Kenilworth station, which finally reopened on 30 April 2018. Planning permission was granted for a single-platform station on the Leamington Spa-Coventry line in 2011. Funding for the project was approved two years later and a target opening date was set for December 2016. However, the construction work did not actually start until July 2016 and the opening date was then deferred no less than four times – the reasons including delays in updating the track and signalling, the non-availability of rolling stock and drivers, and delays with the paperwork relating to safety. The cost of the relatively modest facility was a staggering £11.3 million.

Still under construction on 3 July 2019 was Warrington West station, designed to serve a large area of housing and industry on the outskirts of Warrington. Unit 195120 passes through on a test train. (*Paul Shannon*)

CHAPTER 3

FREIGHT TERMINALS

'Fewer, bigger and more specialised' would make a fair summary of freight terminal trends since 1970. In reality these trends go back a long time. When the railways were first built, almost every passenger station was accompanied by its own goods yard, often with a shed and one or more cranes. Private sidings were numerous and served a wide range of customers, not just those associated with heavy industry. Rationalisation gathered pace in the 1950s and a large-scale cull of both public goods yards and private sidings took place in the mid-1960s, hastened by the publication of the Beeching Report. On the positive side, new contracts signed in the 1960s often resulted in new, specialised terminals being provided, increasingly geared to deliveries in whole trainloads.

By the 1970s, BR had largely concentrated its public freight facilities on larger centres. Essentially there were two types of public freight terminal: those where the railway offered lifting by fixed or mobile crane as well as collection and delivery by road; and those which were just sidings where the customer was responsible for the handling. For each terminal offering collection and delivery, BR defined the area that it served. Some of

Redmire was for many years the loading point for limestone to British Steel Redcar. Air-braked hopper wagons were introduced on this route in the mid-1970s. The loading terminal at Redmire is pictured on 8 August 1977, with one wagon in position for loading and others waiting to be moved by gravity down to the chute. Once loaded, the wagons would be moved again by gravity into the sidings at the west end. This arrangement meant that no pilot locomotive was necessary, nor did the main line locomotive have to run round its train. The limestone flow from Redmire ended in December 1992 when British Steel changed its source to Hardendale in Cumbria. (*Paul Shannon*)

Lincoln coal depot lay on the former Great Central line between St Marks station and Pelham Street crossing. The depot was equipped with apparatus for tipping wagons so that they could discharge their coal through end doors. It survived just long enough to see deliveries in air-braked hoppers via the Speedlink Coal network. 47458 passes the depot with a London King's Cross to Cleethorpes express on 23 August 1978. (*Paul Shannon*)

In the late 1970s, Cambridge Coalfields was still a fully functioning public freight terminal, with BR offering a mobile crane and local collection and delivery by road. All kinds of traffic were handled at Coalfields including seed potatoes, insulation materials, bagged urea and imported fruit. On 11 October 1978, a rake of Borail wagons is being loaded with two unusual types of freight, tractors for export to Ireland via Fishguard and military containers for the army base at Donnington. Within the next few years, the traffic through Coalfields would decline sharply as BR reduced its network of public terminals; however some flows would be able to transfer to the privately owned Potter Group terminal at Ely. (*Paul Shannon*)

The formation of Freightliner in the 1960s effectively separated container traffic from the general freight network, with containers and conventional wagons rarely running in the same train. However, there were a few exceptions, notably in the North of Scotland where containerised whisky was moved by BR instead of Freightliner. 25230 waits at Elgin freight terminal on 25 September 1980 while containers switch modes. The terminal would remain active into the twenty-first century, with seed potatoes being loaded in 2008 and even a trial load of whisky operating in 2013. Unfortunately, as with several Scottish freight trials, rail was ultimately unable to compete with road. (*Paul Shannon*)

BR tried hard to integrate grain traffic into the Speedlink network but struggled to maintain regular volumes from specific locations in order to justify the allocation of resources. A handful of Polybulk grain hoppers awaits loading at the S.C. Banks sidings at Fulbourne, between Cambridge and Bury St Edmunds, on 17 January 1981. This terminal was only used sporadically and fell into disuse during the 1980s. (*Paul Shannon*)

Shunting the Vic Berry scrapyard at Leicester Braunstone Gate on 3 June 1981 is pilot loco 08695. The scrap metal is being carried in 16-ton mineral wagons with no automatic brakes, of the same type that carried coal. Their bodies look to be in similar condition to those piled up awaiting scrapping. BR at that time served dozens of small scrapyards dotted around the network and it would take several years before a programme of rationalisation was complete and all remaining scrap traffic moved in air-braked wagons. (*Paul Shannon*)

Among the numerous sources of coal traffic in South Wales was Abercwmboi Phurnacite plant in the Cynon valley. It took train-loads of coal from local pits and dispatched wagonloads of Phurnacite – smokeless fuel briquettes – to distribution depots across the country. Both types of traffic are illustrated in this view dated 14 April 1982. On the right, 37225 departs from Abercwmboi with empty MDO and HTO wagons for Lady Windsor colliery, while on the left, 37300 is hooked up to a train of Phurnacite for Radyr yard. The Phurnacite traffic tailed off sharply in the late 1980s as BR slimmed down its network of coal depots and the Abercwmboi plant closed completely in 1991. (*Paul Shannon*)

At Oxford, this unusual swing bridge gave access to Rewley Road station which had been the 1851 terminus of the LNWR line from Bletchley. Passenger services were transferred to the main ex-GWR station in 1951, but coal traffic continued until 1984. Pilot loco 08803 is in charge of the Rewley Road duty in March 1983 and is about to position three 16-ton mineral wagons in the coal yard. (*Michael Rhodes*)

Harworth colliery retained its traditional exchange sidings for wagonload traffic in the early 1980s even though much of the coal moved in fixed-formation merry-go-round trains. 20208 and 20133 depart from Harworth with the 6T64 trip working to Worksop sidings on 13 April 1983. The track on the right had nothing to do with the colliery; rather it served Harworth Glass Bulbs factory. (*Paul Shannon*)

Birkenhead Docks turned out to be one of the last places on the network where Class 03 shunters could be seen in action. A minor revival in the early 1980s saw deliveries of grain, coal, steel and paraffin using the sharply curved dock lines. 03189 shunts grain and coal together at one of the flour mills on 6 July 1983. The last traffic to remain on rail at Birkenhead Docks was coal, which continued until the early 1990s. Rumours of a possible rail revival in the twenty-first century have so far come to nothing. (*Paul Shannon*)

Lakeland opencast disposal point near Maryport gained rapid loading facilities in 1980/81, enabling it to handle merry-go-round trains. They were mostly bound for Fiddlers Ferry power station or Workington Docks for export. 40129 arrives at the terminal with 6P49, the 0655 empties from Workington, on 13 July 1983. The disposal point would remain in use for another decade, finishing with a short-term flow to Padiham in 1993. (*Paul Shannon*)

those areas were large: Luton Crescent Road for example offered deliveries as far as Watford, Wellingborough and Northampton, while Shrewsbury served much of mid-Wales including the Cambrian Coast.

In 1981, BR still provided cranage, collection and delivery at 74 terminals. The list ranged from Fort William with its modest four-tonne crane to major steel terminals such as Wolverhampton which could lift up to 40 tonnes and Sheffield up to 35 tonnes. Two entries that stand out from the list are Valley on the Isle of Anglesey and Bridgwater, both with 56-tonne cranes. Those two terminals were specially equipped for nuclear flask traffic but could handle other freight as required. A number of terminals offering cranage were located at ports, including Birkenhead, Fishguard, Heysham, Liverpool, Newhaven, Port Glasgow, Stranraer and Tilbury.

The second category of public freight terminals – basically sidings with road access – still ran into the hundreds in the 1970s, despite the rationalisation of the previous decade. Some were available for any type of traffic, whereas others handled coal and smokeless fuels only. The coverage across the network was uneven and depended on various factors such as the presence of local customers and, especially in built-up areas, the attractiveness of the land for redevelopment. The list still included some locations where traffic had long since fizzled out but BR had not gone through the official closure process.

Looking at typical examples, on the West Coast main line between London Euston and Rugby, public sidings were available in 1981 at Watford, Bletchley, Northampton and Rugby. On the commuter lines south of London, sidings were located at South Lambeth, Norwood Junction, Redhill, Guildford and Rochester – a short list compared with the dozens of passenger stations in the area. The North Wales Coast line was more generously catered for, with sidings at Rhyl, Colwyn Bay, Llandudno Junction, Bangor, Gaerwen and Valley. Even better provision was found on the Far North line, with total of 15 public freight sidings between Inverness and Thurso inclusive.

The Barrow-in-Furness Docks branch served two coal depots in the early 1980s. 25221 shunts the very basic facilities at Hackett depot on 14 July 1983. After completing its duties here, it would reverse further down the branch to shunt Cart depot. Rail deliveries to the two depots ceased shortly after the date of this photograph, but the branch did not officially close until 1989. (*Paul Shannon*)

The massive railway goods warehouse at Bolton Trinity Street was still standing on 23 May 1984 when 31149 was captured shunting steel wagons in the yard. Freight traffic had moved to Trinity Street after the Halliwell Goods branch closed in 1981. However, neither the warehouse nor the sidings at Trinity Street would last much longer, as the land was to be sold off for redevelopment. Wagonload freight for the Bolton area was diverted to Ardwick West terminal until that too closed in 1990. (*Paul Shannon*)

During the 1980s, BR progressively reduced its network of public freight terminals. Some closures were driven by the withdrawal of local trip workings which made a disproportionately high use of resources. Others were simply the result of reduced traffic. Among the major terminals which closed were Park Royal – the last fully equipped public freight terminal in West London – in 1982, Bradford Valley in 1984 and Leeds Whitehall Road in 1990. At the other end of the scale, the last four coal depots on the Cambrian Coast line officially closed in 1983 – although in practice, deliveries had ceased when BR suspended traffic over Barmouth Bridge in 1980. The list of coal depots would shrink further in 1984, when BR closed down its traditional wagonload network in favour of the more specialised Speedlink operation.

The rundown of public freight terminals managed directly by BR came to a rapid conclusion in July 1991 when Speedlink was abandoned. If all rail freight moved in complete trainloads, then there was no place for general purpose terminals geared to small quantities of traffic. Officially, BR withdrew not only from cranage, collection and delivery – in those few locations where it was still on offer – but also from wagonload traffic to and from unstaffed public sidings. In reality, the closure plans eluded two terminals – Birmingham Landor Street and Longport – which continued to operate under railway management into the twenty-first century. There was also a brief revival of wagonload traffic in the mid-1990s, which led to a number of former station goods yards coming back into use for loading timber.

While BR was cutting its wagonload freight provision, private operators went some way towards plugging the gap. The 1980s saw the setting up and expansion of a number of private distribution railheads.

Beeston near Nottingham was one of the smaller Freightliner depots which succumbed to the cutbacks of the mid-1980s. In later years it had been served by a feeder working to and from Birmingham Landor Street as it could not produce enough traffic of its own to justify a direct trunk service. 31167 departs from Beeston with 4G50, the 1523 feeder to Landor Street, on 27 July 1984. The site of Beeston Freightliner terminal has since become a railway infrastructure depot. (*Paul Shannon*)

The Bickershaw branch south of Wigan was latterly worked as a three mile long siding from Springs Branch, with no run round loop at its end. This meant that all trains had to be topped and tailed, often using two pairs of Class 20s. Locos 20070 and 20026 are positioned at the Wigan end of a train from Fiddlers Ferry on 27 March 1985 while loading takes place. By that time, coal was brought to the surface at just two locations in Lancashire, Bickershaw and Parkside. The traffic from Bickershaw would continue until 1992. (*Paul Shannon*)

Nuclear flasks require special handling equipment and from the 1960s BR established dedicated terminals for flask traffic on the nearest convenient stretch of railway to each power station. For Trawsfynydd this meant reopening a seven-mile stretch of the ex-GWR line from Blaenau Ffestiniog and installing a terminal near the former Trawsfynydd Lake halt. A flask has just been lifted on to its wagon on 17 April 1985, ready to be collected by a Class 25 loco for the first stage of its journey to Sellafield. Trawsfynydd power station was shut down in 1991 and the last nuclear flask train from the terminal ran in April 1997. (*Paul Shannon*)

The station goods yard at Northenden became a Blue Circle cement terminal after its closure to general freight in the 1960s. It was a compact site with no headshunt, which meant that wagons had to be left on the main line during shunting operations. 25051 and 25200 stand at Northenden on 28 May 1985 awaiting permission to move out of the siding. The cement terminal closed in 2000 in favour of a new railhead at Weaste, but the sidings at Northenden were then used to receive occasional trainloads of limestone from Dowlow until 2015. (*Paul Shannon*)

The Stranraer railhead of Stockton Haulage is pictured on 25 July 1985, with 47211 waiting while steel girders are unloaded from a BDA wagon. Stockton Haulage had adopted Stranraer as a railhead for export traffic from Teesside to Northern Ireland a few years earlier, having secured Scotland's first Government Section 8 Grant for new or improved rail freight facilities. In 1985, three trains a day ran to the railhead, although overall tonnages were low because of the severe gradients on the line from Ayr. The operation came to an end in 1994 because of the high haulage costs per tonne moved. (*Paul Shannon*)

In the 1980s, the Port of Workington used its modern discharge terminal to offload coal from Maryport for loading into adjacent ships. The main destinations were Ireland and Spain. 47372 draws its rake of 30 HAA merry-go-round hoppers through the terminal on 30 July 1985 before returning to Maryport for the second load of the day. The coal facility died with the end of Cumbrian coal mining in the early 1990s, but the rails into the docks have remained in use for other traffic, latterly calcium carbonate from Aberdeen. (*Paul Shannon*)

Long after its closure to passengers, a section of the former Tanat Valley line near the Wales-England border remained in use for ballast trains from Blodwell quarry into the 1980s. 25042 has just arrived from Bescot with empty wagons on 21 August 1985. The operation ceased in October 1989, but the line was not officially closed for another four years. The loading equipment at Blodwell was dismantled in 2008. (*Paul Shannon*)

Isolated sections of the Manchester Ship Canal Railway survived at various locations after the main route alongside the canal became disused. At Weaste, the MSC was responsible for shunting the Lancashire Tar Distillers terminal, where two of its Sentinel locomotives, DH23 and DH24, are seen in action on 28 August 1985. The terminal received tank trains from Port Clarence at that time. Rail-borne deliveries to Weaste ceased in June 1998, although two years later, the short branch from Eccles returned to use for Blue Circle cement traffic. (*Paul Shannon*)

The station goods yard at Gathurst between Wigan and Southport became a specialised terminal for explosives from the nearby Nobel factory. 25192 calls at Gathurst to exchange empty for loaded vans on 29 August 1985. The vehicle immediately behind the locomotive is a former ferry van redeployed as a barrier vehicle. The shed on the right had once been the starting point of a narrow gauge railway to the factory, but this was replaced by road transport in the late 1970s. (*Paul Shannon*)

Ashington in Northumberland was home to one of the most fascinating rail freight operations in the country. Alongside the main line trains, the National Coal Board relied heavily on rail for local movements of coal for stocking and shale for dumping. For that purpose, it maintained more than a dozen ex-BR Class 14 loco-motives and a large fleet of wooden bodied wagons. One of the former Class 14s is parked on the right as 37084 runs round a brake van at Ashington on 17 July 1986. By the end of that year, the system was no more. (*Paul Shannon*)

A short section of the former Midhurst line was revived in 1972 to carry gravel from Lavant. Using a small fleet of unique side-discharge hopper wagons, the trains travelled just five miles to Drayton, near Chichester, where the gravel was emptied into a lagoon and later retrieved once the water had removed unwanted clay. 73121 waits at Lavant on 18 August 1987 while its train is loaded, an operation which took just a few minutes thanks to an overhead tripper system. The traffic ceased in 1991. (*Paul Shannon*)

The china clay discharge terminal at Carne Point, Fowey, is pictured on 16 February 1988, shortly after the facility had been rebuilt to cater for a new generation of rolling stock, the air-braked CDA hoppers. Until the previous month, the Fowey clay traffic had used ageing wooden-bodied wagons that were in urgent need of replacement. During the past 30 years, Cornish clay operations have been scaled down, but Fowey was still receiving one or two trainloads a day in late 2018. (*Paul Shannon*)

The building of the Channel Tunnel generated much rail freight. At Shakespeare Cliff, between Dover and Folkestone, reclaimed land was used as a railhead for deliveries of concrete tunnel segments. Pilot loco 09024 is shunting two PXA and two POA wagons carrying segments on 21 August 1989. Next to the locomotive is a Southern Railway design brake van and running across the middle of the photograph are the 900mm gauge tracks that connected with the tunnel itself. Once the construction project was complete, the area pictured here became Samphire Hoe Country Park. (*Paul Shannon*)

The Steetley chemical plant at West Ham, located alongside the North Woolwich branch, received wagonloads of sulphuric acid from Avonmouth. The wagons were tripped from Temple Mills yard and had to be propelled into the terminal from the run round loop at Stratford Market. 37053 is in charge of the early morning arrival on 24 August 1989. The plant closed in the following year. (*Paul Shannon*)

The Potter Group was one of the first companies to enter the market, opening its first rail terminal at Ely in 1981 and its second at Selby in 1983. Another successful private railhead was the Fogarty terminal at Blackburn, extended with Government Section 8 Grant assistance in 1983 to handle a range of traffics including steel, china clay, paper and timber. In Scotland, J.G. Russell and P.D. Stirling established sizeable distribution depots at Deanside and Mossend respectively. These two facilities, plus the previously established terminal at Law Junction, took over the role of BR's Glasgow High Street freight depot.

A good number of private distribution railheads survived into the 1990s and, in a few cases, even longer. Those that enjoyed a regular service in 1995 included Aberdeen, Deanside, Mossend, Blackburn, Bamber Bridge, Wakefield, Ely, Cardiff Canton, Avonmouth, Oxford Cowley, Stratford and Gidea Park. Among the typical traffic flows were imported mineral water, paper, chipboard, fertiliser and steel. One of the last private distribution railheads to open was Knowsley, operated by the Potter Group. It began receiving paper from Immingham by rail in 2001 and handled occasional deliveries of other goods from mainland Europe.

As EWS scaled down its revival of wagonload traffic in the early 2000s, so the network of private distribution railheads shrank, recalling the mass closure of public freight terminals a decade earlier. Much of the business handled at the private railheads came from mainland Europe and was severely disrupted by problems with the Channel Tunnel, including the mass entry of asylum seekers to the UK in 2001. That disruption caused the closure of Ordsall Lane and Cardiff Canton depots and deprived several others of valuable traffic. Today, the few distribution depots that remain handle only traffic in full trainloads, such as aggregates to the Potter Group at Ely and steel to P.D. Stirling at Mossend.

Re-reading the 1963 Beeching Report, the eventual demise of the general purpose terminal handling freight in single wagons should perhaps come as no surprise.

Ciba-Geigy installed a rail connection into its Duxford chemicals plant in 1980 so that it could increase its use of rail freight. Previously, it had relied on road connections from railheads at Whittlesford, Great Chesterford and Cambridge Coalfields. A rake of JIA/JIB urea hoppers is being shunted at Duxford by the resident Mercedes Unimog road-rail vehicle on 26 July 1991. On the left is the company's Unilok machine, built by Hugo Aeckerle & Co. (*Paul Shannon*)

Complex shunting operations returned to Melton Mowbray goods yard in 1991 when Pedigree Petfoods began using Charterail Piggyback trailers to move its product to Cricklewood and Glasgow Deanside. Pedigree Petfoods had previously loaded containers on to rail wagons in the goods loop just east of the station. 20195 provides shunting traction at Melton Mowbray on 2 January 1992. Unfortunately, the operation came to an abrupt end in August 1992 when Charterail collapsed. Later efforts to find new uses for the Piggyback equipment were unsuccessful. (*Paul Shannon*)

What was also expected to happen was the transfer of wagonload traffic to containers, with a network of strategic railheads dotted around the country but far fewer in number than the old-style freight terminals. In fact, container traffic grew rapidly in the 1970s, although not quite in the way that had been foreseen.

The launch of the first Freightliner service in 1965 saw the first two dedicated container terminals added to the BR map – Glasgow Gushetfaulds and Maiden Lane in North London. By 1968, Freightliner was serving 17 terminals, most of which were equipped with gantry cranes for the efficient handling of International Standards Organisation containers. The network continued to grow in the 1970s but was increasingly geared to deep-sea boxes rather than domestic freight distribution. Tilbury Freightliner terminal opened in 1970, and both Southampton and Felixstowe gained dedicated terminals for rail-borne containers in 1972. At its peak in the mid-1980s the Freightliner network served 35 locations, including some third party sites such as Containerbase at Aintree and Manchester Barton Dock.

The cost and time penalties of road-rail transfer meant that Freightliner carried less and less domestic traffic. Those terminals that dealt mainly with domestic containers

After the demise of Speedlink the Otis distribution terminal at Ordsall Lane, Salford, became the destination for a daily train of Guinness from Park Royal. New trackwork and a new transhipment shed were provided for the traffic, which was delivered by road to customers throughout northern England and North Wales. 47227 departs from Ordsall Lane with empty vans for Park Royal on 6 January 1992, while on the other side of the fence three railhead staff deliberate over a slight mishap. (*Paul Shannon*)

King's Cross Goods occupied a large site just north of King's Cross passenger terminus. In its later years, it handled cement and various grades of aggregates. 08709 shunts hopper wagons in the Tarmac Topmix sidings on 17 February 1992. The wagons had delivered sea-dredged aggregate from Angerstein Wharf on the south bank of the Thames. The site of King's Cross Goods would later be swallowed up by High Speed 1 construction works, but a replacement terminal for cement and aggregates would be provided at Churchyard Sidings just outside St Pancras. (*Paul Shannon*)

Hunterston deep water terminal was built in the late 1970s to transfer imported iron ore and coal to rail wagons for the 51-mile journey to Ravenscraig steelworks. Hunterston replaced an earlier facility at General Terminus Quay, which had become unsuitable for increasingly large vessels. For most of their duration, the Hunterston-Ravenscraig ore trains used pairs of Class 37 locomotives, with a third locomotive added for the 1 in 77 climb between Mossend and Holytown, but towards the end, single Class 60s took over. 60050 has almost finished drawing its train through the loading bunker at Hunterston before forming 6D14 to Ravenscraig on 15 April 1992. The ore traffic finished when Ravenscraig closed, but the deep-water terminal then returned to use for coal to Scottish and English power stations. This too finished in April 2017, and the loading facility has since been dismantled. (*Paul Shannon*)

The Port of Liverpool rail terminal at Seaforth opened in 1979, not long after conventional rail freight in the docks area had ceased. For a time, it was busy with Freightliner traffic and trainloads of containerised coal for export, but volumes declined and all that remained by late 2008 was a weekly delivery of stainless steel from Tinsley. On 30 October 1992, Trainload Coal liveried loco 37222 provides unusual traction for the lunchtime feeder service to Garston. In May 2018 DB Cargo made a fresh attempt to carry containers by rail from Seaforth, with a three times weekly service to Mossend. (*Paul Shannon*)

Flows of sea-dredged aggregates from the Thames estuary began using air-braked hopper wagons as early as 1968. The traffic from Angerstein Wharf used special high-floor wagons so that the load could be discharged through hopper doors on to a mobile conveyor inserted underneath. That saved the expense of installing fixed hopper discharge equipment at each receiving terminal. The conveyor is pictured in action at Paddington on 17 February 1993, while 60039 waits at the head of the train. Other terminals equipped in this way were King's Cross, Battersea and Park Royal. (*Paul Shannon*)

The official opening of Wakefield Europort took place on 8 January 1996. The Managing Director of Railfreight Distribution delivers a speech in front of invited guests and officials as 47287 waits to depart with a train of mainly empty containers. Unfortunately, Wakefield Europort never attracted worthwhile volumes of Channel Tunnel traffic, although it has kept going into the twenty-first century as a railhead for deep-sea containers. (*Paul Shannon*)

Alongside the modern handling facilities at Wolverhampton Steel Terminal are the remains of the Chillington Wharf basin, originally built in 1820 to tranship products from the Chillington Iron Company into canal boats and adapted for railway use in 1902. Steel billet awaits unloading beside the basin on 27 May 1998. At that time, Wolverhampton Steel Terminal was receiving up to eight trains a day delivering various types of semi-finished and finished steel as well as aluminium billet. Today it handles fewer trains, but tonnages remain high. (*Paul Shannon*)

Liverpool Bulk Terminal was one of several port railheads built as an indirect result of the demise of coal mining in the UK. It opened in August 1993, supplying coal mainly for Fiddlers Ferry power station. However, over time the terminal served other customers including Castle Cement at Penyffordd and Clitheroe. 66014 draws forward under the loader with MEA wagons which will later form 6P82, the 1430 departure to Clitheroe, on 1 June 1999. The coal from Liverpool Bulk Terminal ceased in summer 2015, but the port now loads biomass on to rail for movement to Drax. (*Paul Shannon*)

The O'Connor Group established an intermodal terminal on the former British Oxygen Company site at Widnes in 1998. In the early stages, the terminal handled both trainload business for Freightliner and wagonload traffic for EWS. 47370 shunts Freightliner traffic at the terminal on 12 July 1999 before departing with 4F02, the 1710 feeder service to Garston. Traffic built up rapidly and the operator later installed an overhead gantry crane to make the terminal run more efficiently. It now specialises in deep-sea traffic to and from Felixstowe and Southampton. (*Paul Shannon*)

Associated British Ports and British Steel provided Newport Docks with a rail-connected covered terminal in 1998, partly funded by a substantial Freight Facilities Grant from the Welsh Office. It housed two 40-tonne gantry cranes and offered 53,800sqft of storage space. The terminal handled coil from Llanwern for export as well as longer-distance flows. 09105 shunts BYA steel carriers at Newport Docks on 26 October 2000. (*Paul Shannon*)

were vulnerable. King's Cross and Dudley both closed in 1986 and eight further terminals were culled in 1987. Scotland was particularly hard hit, losing its Freightliner presence at Aberdeen, Dundee and Edinburgh and retaining only Coatbridge and Glasgow Gushetfaulds. Meanwhile, investment was made in the core network for deep-sea traffic: The original terminal at Felixstowe was joined by a second terminal – Felixstowe North – in 1983, and Stockton was replaced by a better facility at Wilton in 1989. Thamesport joined the Freightliner network in 1991. On the other hand, domestic container traffic continued to decline; the two London terminals at Willesden and Stratford closed in 1992 and 1994 respectively.

A new focus for container terminals in the 1990s was the Channel Tunnel. With most freight through the Tunnel expected to travel in containers, BR's Railfreight Distribution arm set up a network of inland terminals, ranging from new sites to the shared use of existing facilities. When the Tunnel opened for business in 1994, three new terminals were available at Willesden, Trafford Park and Mossend, along with four existing Freightliner terminals. Further dedicated terminals were opened at Wakefield in 1996 and at Daventry and Hams Hall in 1997.

Unfortunately, Channel Tunnel rail freight failed to grow as expected and intermodal carryings declined

Dean Lane was one of four rail-served waste transfer stations that were established in Greater Manchester from 1981 onwards. The waste has been sent to a number of destinations; it went mainly to Appley Bridge on the Southport line until 1993, then mainly to Roxby near Scunthorpe until 2014, and since then mainly to Runcorn with occasional trains to Oxwellmains. The haulage contract switched to Freightliner in 2009 when that company signed a 25-year deal with waste contractor Viridor. Back in EWS days, 66122 waits at Dean Lane on 1 August 2001 while its train is reloaded. (*Paul Shannon*)

from the early 2000s onwards. Wakefield, Trafford Park and Hams Hall found themselves redefined as deep-sea container terminals and Willesden was closed altogether. Daventry remained busy, but now with a mixture of maritime business and traffic to and from Scotland. The last Channel Tunnel service carrying general container traffic was a service between Hams Hall and Domodossola, which ceased in 2016.

Today, the railway still serves around 25 container terminals, but their geographical distribution is different from that of the 1970s. Alongside the busy port terminals at Felixstowe, Southampton and – since 2013

– London Gateway, there are clusters of inland facilities for deep-sea traffic in the West Midlands, North West England and Yorkshire, as well as outlying terminals at Wentloog in South Wales and Bristol. Smaller port terminals are active at Tilbury, Purfleet, Tees and Liverpool Seaforth. In Scotland, the container terminals at Mossend, Coatbridge, Grangemouth, Aberdeen and Inverness handle domestic as well as deep-sea traffic. At the newer locations, there has been a trend away from fixed gantry cranes in favour of using mobile lifting equipment, which reduces start-up costs and makes operations more flexible.

Trafford Park Euroterminal was built adjacent to, but separate from, the earlier Freightliner terminal. It was one of three railway-owned terminals that catered for European intermodal traffic from the opening of the Channel Tunnel in 1994, the others being Willesden and Mossend. The five loading sidings at Trafford Park are pictured on 17 February 2003. By that time the terminal was handling domestic as well as European traffic, and gradually the balance would shift further away from the Channel Tunnel in favour of deep-sea boxes. Trafford Park handled its last Channel Tunnel business in 2012. (*Paul Shannon*)

The Smallshaws coal depot at Gobowen was established in 1971 on the site of the former goods yard. It received wagonloads of coal from many different collieries and smokeless fuel plants. It lasted far longer than most other facilities of its type and still accepted occasional deliveries in two-axle HEA wagons as late as 2004. The conveyor system and storage bunkers are pictured on 3 April 2005. (*Paul Shannon*)

Conspicuous by their absence today are the various bi-modal systems that were introduced or trialled in the late twentieth century, such as Roadrailer and Charterail Piggyback. For a time, bi-modal equipment carried parcels between Willesden and Mossend, paper from Aberdeen to Northampton and pet food from Melton Mowbray to Cricklewood and Glasgow Deanside. Although they appear to offer advantages, these systems ultimately failed because of their high cost and lack of flexibility. The restricted loading gauge of the British network is also a limiting factor.

For bulk freight, the railway has provided increasingly specialised terminals since the 1960s, coinciding with the growth of trainload operation. Today, most bulk freight terminals handle only one type of traffic, usually on behalf of a single customer. In some cases, old terminals have been given a new purpose – such as several former station goods yards in South East England which are now aggregates terminals – but factors such as siding length and road access mean that repurposing is not always practicable.

Coal is perhaps more closely associated with the railway than any other type of freight. In the 1970s, some domestic coal depots had hopper discharge equipment, while others were simply sidings from which coal was unloaded by shovel. Power station coal and some flows to other large customers were increasingly handled in merry-go-round wagons, which required automated facilities at both ends of the route to allow loading and discharge on the move. Today, the few coal trains that remain still use automated discharge, but the loading at ports is often by mechanical shovel rather than from an overhead bunker. For biomass traffic, the fine nature of the material means that both loading and discharge have to take place in carefully controlled conditions, avoiding moisture and wind.

Bromford Bridge was one of the last rail-served bitumen terminals in the country. It received its supplies in two-axle tank wagons from Fawley refinery. For a time EWS ran a combined train from Fawley to the West Midlands which conveyed liquefied petroleum gas for Longport and gas oil for railway fuelling points as well as the bitumen; however, by 2004 only the bitumen remained and it ran as a twice-weekly block train. The Bromford Bridge terminal is pictured on 17 December 2008, shortly before its closure. (*Paul Shannon*)

At the start of 1970, Felixstowe was a relatively minor location on the rail freight map and trains had to reverse at Felixstowe Town station in order to gain access to the port. Today, three rail-served container terminals – opened in 1972, 1983 and 2013 respectively – make the port one of the busiest rail freight locations in the country, with more than 30 scheduled departures a day. 66517 stands at the 1983 Felixstowe North terminal having just arrived light engine from Felixstowe South on 7 April 2010. (*Paul Shannon*)

As with coal, terminals for aggregates traffic – stone, gravel and sand – range from simple to sophisticated. The busiest loading terminals such as Merehead, Whatley and Mountsorrel tend to have automated loading equipment, but this is not universal: The new terminal at Arcow for example uses mechanical shovels instead. At the other end of the journey, some terminals are equipped for hopper discharge, while others again rely on mechanical shovels. Some of the newer facilities fall into the latter category, avoiding the expense and complication of installing a conveyor and providing greater flexibility if a change of use is required.

An interesting episode was the rise and fall of the Self Discharge Train, designed to enable a trainload of hopper wagons to discharge its load by means of a continuous conveyor belt at solebar level and an extendable boom that could be positioned at right angles to the train. The Self Discharge Train was introduced in 1988 and operated successfully for many years; however, an accident with the extendable boom caused the instant withdrawal of the technology in February 2016.

Many cement terminals were established in the 1960s and 1970s as regional distribution points for specific producers. The traffic declined sharply in the 1990s in favour of direct road deliveries to the end customer, but has recovered in the last two decades, with new railheads established at locations such as Moorswater, Seaham, West Thurrock and Dagenham.

Much steel traffic runs between terminals that are within major steel plants and therefore not managed by the railway as such. However, the railway still serves a small number of steel terminals for general storage and

The nineteenth century goods shed at Blackburn was one of the last of its type to be used for its original purpose of offloading rail freight under cover. In later years, it formed part of the distribution terminal that was set up by Fogarty's in the 1970s. Its last regular wagonload flow was imported chipboard from Menznau, Switzerland, which ceased in 2010. 66020 is propelling three vanloads of chipboard into the shed on 3 June 2010 having worked 6N42, the 0838 departure from Warrington Arpley. The terminal has since handled one trial load of steel and a few outgoing stone trains, but its days as a general distribution railhead are over. (*Paul Shannon*)

In January 2016, Tarmac opened its Arcow terminal to load gritstone from Arcow and Dry Rigg quarries, bringing a welcome boost to the Settle and Carlisle line. Trains have so far run mainly to Leeds Hunslet, Bredbury and Pendleton, with GB Railfreight locomotives hauling various types of rolling stock. Loaded trains run north to Blea Moor to run round before heading back south. 66749 shunts former coal hoppers at Arcow on 26 May 2017 before working 6M37, the 1113 departure to Pendleton. (*Paul Shannon*)

distribution, such as Rotherham Masborough, Round Oak and Wolverhampton. In the past, the list of terminals handling steel was much longer, including five dedicated terminals in the West Midlands alone, but these days the operation is concentrated on a small number of locations because regular trainload quantities are required and much of the steel needs to be loaded and unloaded under cover.

The movement of scrap metal has changed from a large number of mainly small operations to a small number of high-volume flows. In the 1970s, scrap was loaded in some station goods yards and at a few larger sites that often had their own internal railway systems. The last examples of the latter were Shipley and Stockton, both now abandoned. Those scrap terminals that remain in use today are basically simple sidings alongside a loading pad.

Chemicals and petroleum require special handling and in the 1970s the railway delivered these products to many locations, both for specific end users and for general distribution. Areas such as Teesside, Humberside and the Mersey estuary once boasted clusters of chemical plants that had specialised facilities for rail-borne chemicals, ranging from caustic soda and sulphuric acid to liquid chlorine and anhydrous ammonia. Today, the traffic has almost all gone; the last remaining loading terminal for chemicals traffic is the Ineos Chlor siding at Runcorn Folly Lane, opened in 2002.

The number of petroleum terminals has also fallen, but less dramatically than for chemicals. Many petroleum railheads were established in the 1960s when BR signed contracts with major suppliers for bulk

Biomass has produced useful volumes of rail freight, albeit on a restricted number of routes. Immingham is one of four ports where biomass has been put on rail for delivery to Drax, the others being Liverpool, Tyne and Hull. The massive biomass loading point at Immingham is pictured on 27 September 2017 as 66152 – the first ex-EWS loco to carry DB livery – departs with 6H77, the 1615 to Drax. It will run round in the loop on the Killingholme branch before heading back past the terminal. Apart from the Drax flows, biomass is also moved by rail from the Port of Tyne to Lynemouth power station. (*Paul Shannon*)

After several years of planning and construction, Doncaster Iport welcomed its first regular train service in September 2018, a GB Railfreight-hauled working from Southampton. The terminal is located on the freight-only line to Worksop via Maltby, which means that it is difficult to reach from the East Coast main line; therefore, the trains are routed in both directions via Chesterfield and Rotherham. 66715 departs from Doncaster Iport with 4O33, the 1804 train to Southampton Western Docks, on 11 October 2018. Business built up quickly and services to and from Tees and Felixstowe were introduced in 2019. (*Paul Shannon*)

deliveries. The receiving terminals ranged in size from the huge complex at Leeds which took several trainloads a day to the small facility at Shrewsbury Abbey, reached by a wagonload trip working. Today, the railway serves around a dozen petroleum terminals, of which the busiest are Westerleigh, Theale, Kingsbury and Dalston. As with other types of rail freight, the costs of running a petroleum railhead can be prohibitive compared with direct road deliveries from the refinery to the end customer. Pipelines have also put paid to some former rail flows, while tighter emissions regulations have led to terminal closures because the necessary upgrade would be too expensive.

CHAPTER 4

DEPOTS AND YARDS

In 1970, the BR traction fleet still depended on a large number of maintenance depots, located at strategic points across the network, and a smaller number of engineering works for major repairs and modifications. This was essentially a slimmed down version of the steam age model, where locomotives returned to their home shed for routine attention and made periodic visits to works.

Over the last forty years that model has gradually given way to a more flexible system. The division of BR into sectors and sub-sectors in the 1980s brought about a change in how locomotives were allocated to depots. Rather than covering the needs of a particular geographical area, depots began to be associated more with particular types of traffic. At the same time, locomotives and other motive power made less frequent

visits to depots; fuelling was increasingly carried out at locations other than depots, sometimes using a road tanker instead of a fixed installation. The result was that fewer depots were necessary. Since depots did not add any value to the product, closures were welcome.

Another factor that led to the decline of traditional depots was the large reduction in the locomotive fleet, caused partly by freight trains becoming fewer in number and partly by the replacement of most locomotive-hauled passenger trains by units.

Taking the Western Region as an example, in 1970 main line locomotives were allocated to six depots: Old Oak Common; Bristol Bath Road; Cardiff Canton; Landore; Newton Abbot; and Plymouth Laira. These depots had all been built or rebuilt for modern traction in the early 1960s. The locomotives from each depot

In the days when all long-distance and some short-distance trains into King's Cross were loco-hauled, the compact stabling point on the west side of the station throat was busy with passenger traction of various kinds. Examples of Classes 31, 47 and 46 are visible in this photograph dated 17 August 1971. The headcodes show the last train worked by each locomotive: for example, 2B66 was a stopping train from Cambridge and 1A15 was an express from Newcastle, while 5D08 would have been the empty stock for an afternoon departure to Cleethorpes. (*Neil Caplan/Online Transport Archive*)

tended to cover a mixture of traffic types and were home to a mixture of main line traction; for example, Bristol Bath Road had members of Classes 22, 35, 37, 46, 47 and 52 on its books (using the post-1973 TOPS classification). Thirteen further depots across the Region had their own allocation of diesel shunters and in some cases DMUs, as well as acting as stabling and servicing points for main line locomotives. This group included Ebbw Junction, Margam and St Blazey.

Today, none of the six big Western Region diesel depots exists in its original form. Old Oak Common locomotive depot closed in 2009, although a 1970s facility for InterCity 125 units remained in use until 2018 and part of the site is now occupied by a brand-new depot for Elizabeth Line stock. Bristol Bath Road was still home to a large pool of InterCity Class 47s in the early 1990s,

but the depot closed completely in 1995. Cardiff Canton remained busy supplying South Wales freight traction in the 1990s, but its locomotive maintenance facility closed in 2004, since when it has been a stabling point. Landore switched from maintaining locomotives to servicing InterCity 125 units but faces an uncertain future because the replacement InterCity Express units will be maintained at nearby Maliphant instead. Newton Abbot was an early casualty, being downgraded in 1970 and closed completely in 1981. Plymouth Laira has changed the least out of the six depots: Although it no longer has a main line locomotive allocation, it still maintains InterCity 125 units and other stock as required.

Elsewhere in the country, several depots that supported numerous locomotive fleets have now closed or been substantially rebuilt. Thornaby depot on Teesside

While BR retained and adapted some steam sheds for diesel traction, that was not the case at Ebbw Junction (Newport), where a new four-road shed replaced the old facility. Although Ebbw Junction had only a modest allocation of its own – mainly Class 08 shunters plus a few Class 25s and the unique Class 53 'Falcon' for a time – it was often host to a dozen or so Cardiff-based Class 37s between duties in the Newport area. At least nine examples are seen in this photograph dated 8 October 1977. Also on shed on that day were eight Class 08 shunters – a reminder of how much shunting remained an essential part of railway operations even after the Beeching cutbacks. (*Michael Rhodes*)

The GWR shed at Chester lost its steam allocation in 1960 and then became a DMU depot. It supplied trains for a wide area including the North Wales Coast, Cambrian lines and the Wirral. Class 128 parcels cars M55995 and M55994 are stabled beside the former GWR building on 12 June 1977, while a Class 101 unit can just be seen inside the shed. At that time, Chester's allocation included the last of the Class 103 Park Royal DMUs along with members of Classes 101, 108, 119, 120 and 128 – plus a few Class 08 shunters. The shed would be demolished in 1999. (*Paul Shannon*)

had an allocation of 81 locomotives in late 1971 and 93 locomotives in summer 1982, but it had outlived its usefulness by the 2000s and became a sad repository for withdrawn traction. The site was demolished in 2011. Eastfield depot in Glasgow was home to more than 100 locomotives in late 1970 but closed in 1993 and was demolished soon afterwards. A smaller depot for units was built on the site in 2005. Crewe Diesel Depot, which once supplied traction for much of the North West, survived into the twenty-first century as a base for EWS (now DB Cargo) locomotives, but then became little more than a graveyard for redundant traction. However, Locomotive Services Ltd have since taken over the Crewe site and have invested in a new carriage shed as well as renovating the old facility.

Alongside the decline of 1960s depots, new facilities have been provided to suit modern needs. Leeds Midland Road was built from scratch on a disused freight terminal site and now takes responsibility for the Freightliner diesel fleet. Depots at Peterborough and Doncaster Roberts Road maintain the GB Railfreight locomotive fleet. Crewe Gresty Bridge has joined Carlisle Kingmoor as a traction maintenance depot for Direct Rail Services. The former goods shed at Longport is now a repair facility for Class 66 locomotives.

With most passenger trains now comprising units rather than hauled stock, a number of new depots have been built to maintain diesel or electric unit fleets. Central Rivers depot near Burton-on-Trent opened in 2001 as a servicing facility for Virgin Voyager units. The old diesel depot site at Doncaster Carr has given way to an entirely new facility for the InterCity Express units coming into use on the East Coast main line. A new Alstom depot at Edge Hill, Liverpool, maintains TransPennine Express units and West Coast Pendolinos. At Ardwick, just outside Manchester Piccadilly, a new depot for TransPennine Express units was completed in 2006 and has since been adapted to maintain electric stock.

In London and the South East, Reading has gained an entirely new depot for Great Western Railway trains - now electric as well as diesel. The expansion of Thameslink has been supported by new depot facilities at Three Bridges and Hornsey. Two depots have been built for Eurostar trains. The first was North Pole International, located near Old Oak Common and used from 1994 until 2007 while Eurostar trains terminated at London Waterloo. The North Pole facility has since been adapted for Great Western InterCity Express trains. The second Eurostar depot, at Temple Mills, was commissioned in 2007 when Eurostar trains began using HS1 to St Pancras.

Coldham Lane depot, Cambridge, was still home to a small pool of Class 03 shunters in the late 1970s. 03016 is pictured in the wagon repair shed on 26 October 1978 coupled to a typical selection of rolling stock of the era – a rebodied HTV coal hopper, an OHV open wagon, a CPV cement tank and a former parcels van in departmental use. Another HTV hopper is visible on the next track. Coldham Lane would lose its last two Class 03s – of which 03016 was one – in December 1978, leaving a pool of Class 08s for shunting at Cambridge, Ely and Bury St Edmunds. (*Paul Shannon*)

Derby Works in the late 1970s was typically home to around 40 locomotives at any one time. Most would be undergoing various levels of repair, but some were destined for scrapping. A visit to the erecting shop on 10 March 1979 finds a trio of Class 25s – 25214, 25123 and 25218 – receiving attention. Derby at that time specialised in Classes 25, 44, 45 and 46, all of which were familiar traction on the Midland main line and its branches. (*Paul Shannon*)

Swindon Works dated back to the 1840s, when the Great Western Railway chose the location as a convenient point more or less half way between London and Bristol. New locomotive construction at Swindon finished in 1965 with the outshopping of the last Class 14 'Teddy Bear', but the works carried on repairing Western Region locomotives and rolling stock, including the diesel hydraulics while they remained in service. By the late 1970s, Class 08 shunters formed the mainstay of Swindon's locomotive work. This scene from 15 March 1979 shows 08528, 08580, 08036 and 08463. (*Paul Shannon*)

Opened in 1964, Tinsley depot was located beside the then new hump marshalling yard and replaced steam sheds at Canklow, Grimesthorpe, Darnall and Millhouses. It could accommodate up to 200 locomotives, including several main line types and the three Class 13 'master and slave' shunters that were unique to Tinsley. When BR was divided into business sectors, Tinsley passed to Railfreight Distribution and became home to a large fleet of Class 47 locomotives used throughout the network. However, as the railway sought to cut its traction maintenance costs, Tinsley became an expensive luxury and it closed completely in 1998. The photograph shows several Class 45s and Class 47s on shed on 23 September 1980, with 45032 nearest the camera. (*Paul Shannon*)

Stratford Works formed part of the huge complex of railway engineering and maintenance facilities located just north of Stratford station. In BR days, the works became known as the Diesel Repair Shop, where modifications were carried out on various types including High Speed Trains and Class 56s. By the 1980s, the works was busy cannibalising redundant locomotives to keep surviving classmates in service. The photograph dated 4 December 1980 shows 31255 and 'Deltic' 55005 undergoing attention; the 'Deltic' had arrived on 18 November for repairs following an altercation with a herd of cows. The works finally closed its doors in March 1991 and its site has since been redeveloped – partly as Stratford International station and partly as a shopping centre. The adjacent engine shed, which once hosted one of the biggest locomotive allocations in the country, lasted until 1997. (*Paul Shannon*)

Located conveniently alongside the Glasgow Queen Street-Edinburgh main line, Eastfield depot dated back to the early twentieth century but was later adapted for diesel traction and became one of British Rail's most important locomotive depots in the 1970s and 1980s. 47712 takes a Glasgow-Edinburgh train past the depot on 26 August 1981, with many examples of Classes 20, 25, 27 and 37 visible. At that time, the depot's total allocation numbered more than 100 locomotives. Eastfield's days were numbered as loco haulage gave way to units on several Scottish routes and as freight traffic continued to decline, and the depot closed in 1992. A smaller facility was opened on the site in 2004 to maintain ScotRail diesel units. (*Paul Shannon*)

Although it never had its own allocation of main line locomotives, Shirebrook diesel depot was a busy servicing location for traction used on coal traffic in the Mansfield area. The depot opened in 1965 on the site of the former station goods yard. By the early 1980s, Class 56s had joined the older classes 20 and 37. A visit on 21 May 1983 finds the depot well filled, with 56098 and 56117 nearest the camera. As the coal industry in Nottinghamshire fared better than in other parts of the country, Shirebrook remained open until September 1996, but the site has since been cleared. (*Paul Shannon*)

Margam depot opened in March 1964 to provide a purpose-built locomotive servicing facility for West Wales freight, including trains to and from Margam yard and the adjacent Port Talbot steelworks. It never had its own allocation of main line locomotives, but several different classes were regularly serviced there. Visible outside the shed on 23 July 1983 are 47087, 08361, 47246, 37247, 45064 and 47066. Margam depot survived into the twenty-first century and saw a temporary increase in work after Cardiff Canton closed in 2004. However, the revival was short-lived and the depot was replaced by more basic facilities in Margam yard in September 2009. (*Paul Shannon*)

Few depots were more specialised than Knottingley, which existed to stable and service the locomotives used on merry-go-round coal trains in and around the Aire Valley. For a time in the 1970s, Knottingley had a specific allocation of Class 47 locomotives, but generally it acted as a sub-shed to other depots such as Tinsley. In recent years, its work has been much reduced, mainly as a result of the decline in coal traffic but also because Knottingley is a DB Cargo depot and much of the remaining coal is hauled by other operators. Back in BR days, on 10 March 1984, Knottingley is host to at least nine Class 56s and two Class 08 shunters. (*Paul Shannon*)

Toton depot on the Nottinghamshire/Derbyshire border was a major facility when it first opened in the early 1960s, supplying traction for the Midland main line and across the East Midlands. Toton strengthened its position as BR and its successors concentrated their loco maintenance on a smaller number of core locations. This 1987 view shows examples of Classes 56, 47, 58, 20, 08 and 31 parked on the north side of the 15-road shed. At that time, more than 250 locomotives were allocated to Toton, including the entire fleet of Class 58s and most of the Class 56s. (*Michael Rhodes*)

The four-road steam shed at Holyhead remained in use for stabling diesel traction until 1989, when it was demolished and replaced by a narrower purpose-built structure. The level tracks of the old depot contrast with the 1 in 93 gradient on the adjacent running lines in this photograph dated 8 April 1988, with a single Class 142 'Pacer' visible. Today, Holyhead carries out maintenance on various types of passenger traction and stock including the Voyager units that run to and from London. (*Paul Shannon*)

Fuelling points were an essential feature of most traction maintenance depots, but in recent decades their number has diminished as some freight operators have turned to fuelling locomotives from road tankers at convenient lineside locations. The fuelling point at Ripple Lane is pictured on 2 August 1990 with Trainload Petroleum locos 37709 and 37893 in attendance. The mainstay of Ripple Lane's work at that time was oil traffic from the two refineries on the Thames Haven branch, but soon most of that traffic would disappear, resulting in the closure of Ripple Lane depot in 1993. (*Paul Shannon*)

The two-road shed at Thornton Junction was built alongside Thornton marshalling yard, which was completed in 1956 on a green field site. The two facilities were designed to handle the large volume of coal and other freight to and from Fife. By the late 1980s, local traffic had declined to a trickle and the few active sidings in the yard were used mainly for stabling stock and for run-round movements. By summer 1990, Thornton Junction depot had an allocation of just three Class 08 shunters, although main line locos were also serviced there. The photograph shows two pairs of Class 20s outside the shed on 27 August 1990. Once it was no longer needed for freight operations, the shed became home to two ex-LNER locos, A4 60009 *Union of South Africa* and K4 61994 *The Great Marquess*, both owned by John Cameron. (*Paul Shannon*)

The trend towards more specialised freight operations in place of a common-user network has led to the relocation of servicing facilities beside major terminals, cutting out the need for light engine movements to and from depots. Railfreight Distribution installed a small depot for maintaining and repairing its Freightliner wagons and locomotives adjacent to Southampton Maritime container terminal. Three Class 47s and several container flats are present at the depot on 6 September 2000, by which time Freightliner was operating as a private company. (*Paul Shannon*)

Willesden depot with its six parallel shed roads was built in the 1960s for the introduction of electric trains to London Euston. For many years, it was home to BR's Class 86, 87 and 90 locomotives while also seeing visits from other electric classes. The depot lost most of its work when hauled stock gave way to Pendolino units on the West Coast main line, the shed not being long enough to take a complete unit. Some of the spare capacity was taken up by GB Railfreight when it started its freight operations in 2001. Today, the facility is operated by Bombardier and known as Willesden Traincare. The photograph dated 24 October 2002 shows recently introduced loco 66712 flanked by two soon-to-be-replaced electrics. (*Paul Shannon*)

After the closure of Gateshead diesel depot in 1991, locomotives and wagons were serviced at the small shed in Tyne Yard. Although Tyne Yard was predominantly a freight location, BR's successor EWS used the shed to carry out a range of work, including a contract with Bombardier to stable and service Voyager units operated by Virgin Cross Country. The shed was also a convenient stabling point for diesel and electric locomotives on mail traffic to and from Low Fell. Visible through the shed doors on 16 July 2003 is one of the Class 47 locomotives that EWS used on mail trains until the introduction of Class 67s. (*Paul Shannon*)

The most westerly and southerly depot in the country is Long Rock, located just short of the Great Western terminus of Penzance. BR provided Long Rock with a new 750-metre maintenance shed in October 1977 in readiness for the introduction of InterCity 125 units, together with additional stabling sidings with overhead gantry lights. Further expansion took place in 2018 to allow Long Rock to take over the maintenance of Night Riviera sleeper trains from Old Oak Common. The 1970s shed is pictured on 18 April 2006 as 66160 departs with empty fuel tanks for St Blazey – Long Rock being one of the few depots that still received fuel by rail at that time. (*Paul Shannon*)

The railway town of Crewe has seen many changes in the last 50 years. Crewe Works is a shadow of its former self and the former BR diesel and electric depots have declined in importance. On the other hand, Direct Rail Services opened its depot at Gresty Bridge in 2007 and the maintenance company LNWR built a new four-road shed next to the existing Crewe Carriage Shed on the east side of the main line in 1999. The LNWR facility is pictured on 7 April 2006, with DRS 20314 and a Class 153 car present. LNWR was sold to Arriva Trains in 2008 and changed its name to Arriva Traincare. (*Paul Shannon*)

Foster Yeoman expanded its Merehead depot in 1985 to provide covered accommodation for its first four Class 59 locomotives which would enter service in February 1986. After the formation of Mendip Rail in 1993, Merehead took on the maintenance of the Class 59s owned by ARC (later Hanson) as well as those owned by Foster Yeoman. Merehead also gained responsibility for the former National Power Class 59s after these were purchased by EWS in 1998. Hanson 59101 *Village of Whatley* is pictured awaiting attention at Merehead on 3 April 2007. (*Paul Shannon*)

LNWR opened its Leeds Midland Road depot on the site of a disused freight terminal in 2003, following its deal to maintain Freightliner Heavy Haul's Class 66 locomotive fleet. The need for a depot in West Yorkshire arose because of the rapid growth of FHH coal traffic to the Aire Valley power stations. The facility was designed to carry out maintenance up to and including the 'C' examination on the 26 or so Freightliner locomotives used on coal trains. The site is pictured from the north on 24 February 2009, with Heavy Haul loco 66602 and Direct Rail Services classmate 66401 awaiting attention. (*Paul Shannon*)

Freightliner Maintenance Limited acquired Leeds Midland Road depot in 2006. This quickly led to an increase in workload as the depot took responsibility for all 71 Class 66s operated by Heavy Haul, carrying out work up to the six-yearly 'F' examination. The depot later took on the maintenance of the Heavy Haul coal wagon fleet and of Freightliner's intermodal locomotives. Freightliner Maintenance Limited also established mobile teams to maintain locomotives and wagons 'in the field'. Back at Midland Road, 66507, 66526 and 66605 are among the locomotives present on 22 August 2011. (*Paul Shannon*)

Like depots, marshalling yards add no value to the service provided by the railway. Rather, they represent an additional cost to the railway and should only exist where absolutely necessary. Since the 1960s, the gradual shift from wagonload to trainload freight has made traditional marshalling yards redundant. Today, the remnants of some yards are still in use for storing wagons and staging trains en route to their destination. The shunting of individual wagons between trains is now largely limited to railway infrastructure traffic such as ballast, sleepers and spoil.

In 1970, most of the marshalling yards built or redeveloped following the 1955 BR Modernisation Plan remained in use, many still with their mechanised hump operation. But their throughput was declining rapidly. Between 1968 and 1972, the amount of freight moved on BR declined from 204 to 179 million tonnes. More significantly, the proportion of wagonload traffic fell in the same period from 69 to 33 per cent, and by 1977 it would be a mere 20 per cent. Although efforts were made to revitalise wagonload freight, notably through Speedlink from the 1970s until 1991 and later through the short-lived EWS Enterprise network, in reality its days were numbered as early as the 1960s, when road transport became a more attractive option for small consignments.

In Scotland, three hump yards at Millerhill, Thornton, Perth remained active in the early 1970s. The throughput at Millerhill took a tumble after the Edinburgh-Carlisle Waverley route closed in 1969, because some of its traffic was rerouted via the West Coast main line and would not need to come anywhere near Millerhill. The up hump at Millerhill closed in 1970 and the down hump in 1983; thereafter a part of the yard handled Speedlink and trainload traffic, but today the few remaining sidings only act as a staging and crew change point. Thornton yard lost its hump in the early 1970s but remained in use as a flat shunted yard until the end of Speedlink in 1991. Perth yard was downgraded in the 1970s and closed completely in the 1980s; its location on the Highland main line meant that it could not easily

handle Aberdeen traffic once the route via Forfar closed in 1967.

The Glasgow area did not have any mechanised hump yards, although plans once existed to build one. Instead, wagons were marshalled at several flat yards, notably Mossend, Cadder and Sighthill. As traffic declined it made sense to concentrate the activity on a single location, and Mossend was the winner, being well located on the Motherwell-Coatbridge line and having plenty of capacity. Wagonload marshalling was withdrawn from Cadder in 1974 and Sighthill in 1981. Mossend remained busy until the demise of Speedlink, when most of the sidings on the up side were removed. The down sidings, mostly single ended, are still in use today for staging and other operational purposes.

Margam hump yard was opened in 1960 and was at that time the most fully automated marshalling yard in Europe. Covering an area of 178 acres and comprising some 33 miles of track, Margam was capable of sorting 4,500 wagons a day and could handle 220 trains in and out during a 24-hour period. The span of 50 sorting sidings is pictured in August 1978, with the control tower visible on the left. The traffic handled at Margam fell rapidly in the 1970s and the hump was closed in 1980. Further contraction was inevitable and in 1986, BR took the decision to replace the yard completely with a more compact 18-track facility on the site of the old Margam Knuckle yard. (*Michael Rhodes*)

The yard complex at Toton was well placed to handle the huge volumes of coal from the Derbyshire and Nottinghamshire coalfields, but also dealt with a wide range of general freight. However, its throughput fell rapidly from the late 1960s after the introduction of merry-go-round coal trains to local power stations. Two liquid chlorine tanks have just breasted the up hump on 13 March 1980, likely to have been on their way to the Courtaulds factory at Spondon. (*Paul Shannon*)

Designed by the Great Central Railway and opened in 1907, Wath was the first purpose-built hump marshalling yard in the UK. Its two fans of 30 sidings each could handle up to 5,000 wagons in a 24-hour period. Wath later became one of the three end points for electric trains on the Woodhead route – the others being Rotherwood and Tinsley – and in the 1970s, the yard handled merry-go-round trains as well as wagonload traffic. On 15 April 1980, shunter 08050 has just arrived with a brake van from Manvers coking plant, while 20059 and 20005 wait to depart with a scrap metal train for Tinsley. (*Paul Shannon*)

It was Dr Beeching himself who opened Tinsley yard in 1965, enabling a smoother passage for the huge volumes of coal, steel and other traffic generated by the industries around Sheffield and Rotherham. With its single hump and total of 88 sidings, Tinsley had a design throughput of 4,000 wagons a day. Perhaps its biggest claim to fame was the trio of Class 13 'master and slave' shunters which had been converted from pairs of Class 08s to avoid the need for double manning. 13001 is pictured between duties on 1 September 1980. It would be withdrawn in 1981, while its classmates 13002 and 13003 would survive until January 1985. (*Paul Shannon*)

Not surprisingly for one of the most densely industrialised areas in the UK, Teesside became the location of one of the country's largest hump yards in the wake of the 1955 Modernisation Plan. The 200-acre complex at Tees Yard opened for business in 1963. Its two humps remained in operation in the 1970s, with wagonloads of coal, scrap metal, steel and chemicals providing regular traffic. However, the shift to trainload operation gradually deprived the yard of its raison d'être. This view of the up sorting sidings on 12 September 1980 appears to show a healthy number of wagons; however, not all would have been carrying revenue-earning traffic. (*Paul Shannon*)

In North West England, Carlisle yard was one of the classic white elephants of the 1955 Modernisation Plan, never used to its capacity because of the rapid fall in traffic. The inevitable rationalisation saw the closure of the down hump in 1971 and the up hump ten years later. A small part of the yard remains in use today and, unlike some former BR yards, it is used by all the main freight operators – DB Cargo, Freightliner, GB Railfreight, Direct Rail Services and Colas. Further south, the Manchester area was served by several small yards including Dewsnap which closed in 1982 and Ashburys which closed in 1987. Wagonload activity for the whole of the Liverpool-Manchester area and some locations further afield was then concentrated on the Warrington yards – Arpley and Walton Old Junction. Today, Arpley is still an operational location, while Walton Old Junction yard

is used for long-term wagon storage. The extensive yard at Crewe Basford Hall has seen mixed fortunes. It closed as a marshalling point in 1972, but then became a base for Freightliner operations, a role which has expanded in the twenty-first century as the Freightliner company has spread its wings to include railway infrastructure traffic.

North East England was served by two major hump yards built in the early 1960s – Tees and Tyne. In 1970, Tees Yard was one of the busiest of its kind in the country, handling huge volumes of freight to and from the local steel, coal and petroleum industries. But, as almost everywhere else, wagonload traffic declined. The up hump ceased operation in 1982 and the down hump three years later. Two fans of sidings in the former up yard remain in use, although mainly for the long-term storage of rolling stock.

Wagon retarders were an essential feature of mechanised hump yards, ensuring that wagons rolled into their siding at an appropriate speed and came to rest in the correct place. Here in Tees Up Yard on 12 September 1980, a trio of coal hoppers rolls over the primary retarder, which was fully automated. The wagons would then pass over one of the six secondary retarders, which were operated by a 'brake man' in the control tower. If the brake man applied too much pressure, then the wagons would stop short and possibly need to be moved by a pilot locomotive; if he applied too little pressure, then the wagons could hit any vehicles already in the siding and possibly cause damage. (*Paul Shannon*)

Severn Tunnel Junction is the natural railway gateway to South Wales and was therefore the obvious location for a marshalling yard. It was the GWR who first developed the location in the 1930s. The throughput at Severn Tunnel Junction remained healthy during the 1970s as operations were diverted from other yards, but eventually the general decline in wagonload freight made retrenchment unavoidable. However, when the yard complex closed completely in November 1987 it still came as a shock. A visit on 2 October 1980 finds 45037 departing from Severn Tunnel Junction with a Carlisle Kingmoor to Eastleigh freight, while examples of Classes 08, 37, 45 and 46 are stabled on the adjacent tracks. (*Michael Rhodes*)

Tyne Yard was the less busy of the two North East yards. Its hump closed in 1985 and Speedlink marshalling finished in 1989. Today Tyne handles mainly railway infrastructure traffic.

Wagonload shunting in Yorkshire was spread between several yards. Tinsley near Sheffield was the busiest, reached by an electrified extension of the Woodhead route as well as lying on the busy north-south axis through Yorkshire. The closure of Woodhead and general decline in steelmaking led to the downsizing of Tinsley. Its hump closed in 1984 and most of the sidings were later taken out of use, leaving just one small fan for local traffic. Healey Mills yard was once busy with trans-Pennine traffic, but it too lost its hump in 1984 before closing as

a wagonload marshalling point altogether in 1989. Wath yard owed its existence to the local coal industry and, like Tinsley, it handled trains routed via Woodhead. Its rundown started in 1981 and the site was completely abandoned in 1986. Doncaster had an extensive yard complex south of the station, with most wagonload shunting concentrated on Belmont. Many of the sidings are still in place and some are used for railway infrastructure traffic. At York, the compact Dringhouses yard closed in 1988. Finally, Scunthorpe West Yard is notable for two reasons: its opening was delayed until 1971, making it the last marshalling yard arising out of the 1955 Modernisation Plan; and it retained hump shunting until 1990, making it the last active hump yard in the country.

Temple Mills yard opened in 1958 to replace a haphazard scattering of yards on the east side of London. It comprised a single fan of 47 sorting sidings and hump, together with the usual reception and departure sidings and two sets of single-ended sidings for sorting local traffic. Temple Mills was one of the first fully automated hump yards in the country, although it was not long before others came on stream. On 4 December 1980, a rake of MXV mineral wagons loaded with scrap metal from Stratford Market rolls off the hump. By this time, the throughput at Temple Mills had fallen from 4,000 wagons a day in 1970 to just 600, and the yard's days were numbered. (*Paul Shannon*)

Millerhill was Scotland's largest marshalling yard. It opened in 1963 and its two 40-track fans could handle 4,000 wagons a day. On 25 March 1981, 26040 shunts Carflat wagons for the 8J25 trip to Bathgate. A brake van waits on the next track and various types of traffic including pipes for the North Sea oil industry are visible in the sorting sidings. Behind the yard is the winding gear of Monktonhall colliery, which survived until 1997 but whose site has since been earmarked for housing development. (*Michael Rhodes*)

Ellesmere Port was one of the dozens of small yards that acted as gathering points for local traffic and fed into the wagonload network via larger yards. The main business at Ellesmere Port was to and from the various petrochemical customers including Shell and Associated Octel, but the sidings were also a stopping point for coal and other traffic for Birkenhead. 08927 shunts a varied rake of wagons on 14 August 1986, while examples of Classes 25, 47 and 56 rest in the yard. Railfreight around Ellesmere Port suffered catastrophic decline in the decades after this photograph, with no revenue-earning traffic at all passing through the town by 2018. (*Paul Shannon*)

The empty shell of the control tower and acres of barren land convey a hint of busier times at Temple Mills as 47157 waits to depart with the evening feeder service to Willesden on 7 July 1988. This small group of sidings had been retained to reduce the number of trip workings that would otherwise have had to cross London to and from Willesden yard. The traffic that passed through Temple Mills in 1988 included carbon dioxide, construction blocks and coal to Bow, various goods to and from London International Freight Terminal, scrap metal from Silvertown, chemicals to Stratford Market, and chipboard and paper to Gidea Park. However, much of that traffic would soon cease or be rerouted, allowing the site of Temple Mills to be redeveloped over time. (*Paul Shannon*)

Healey Mills yard opened in 1963. Its 120 sidings and single hump were designed to handle 4,000 wagons in a 24-hour period and, unlike many other yards of the era, Healey Mills was still operating at capacity in the mid-1970s. It was the growth of merry-go-round coal traffic which signalled the decline of Healey Mills from the late 1970s onwards. The photograph dated 19 August 1988 shows Trainload Coal loco 37308 setting out with 6S67, the 1452 Speedlink Coal train to Gartcosh. Several rakes of merry-go-round hoppers await their next movement, but there is no evidence of any true wagonload traffic. (*Paul Shannon*)

Built on the site of the LNWR Sudbury hump yard, Wembley European Freight Operating Centre was completed in 1993 to act as a focus for freight traffic to and from mainland Europe, which was expected to increase after the opening of the Channel Tunnel. Although it looked like a marshalling yard, Wembley EFOC was designed with portion exchange and stabling in mind rather than full-scale marshalling. However, while the expected semi-trainload inter-modal traffic failed to grow as expected, wagonload traffic both via the Tunnel and within the UK enjoyed a minor revival in the 1990s. A typical selection of freight stock is pictured in the yard on 22 July 1999, with 66129 nearest the camera on a train of Ford car parts. (*Paul Shannon*)

The growth of the EWS Enterprise network for less than trainload traffic led to a small-scale revival of marshalling yards. This included the reopening of Doncaster Belmont yard in May 1998 to provide a more convenient node for South Yorkshire and Humberside. At its height, Belmont was served by trunk trains to Harwich, Wembley, Bescot, Warrington, Tees and Aberdeen, with feeder services running to Selby, Hull, Immingham, Wakefield, Aldwarke and Ely. 08587 is pictured in action at Belmont on 24 April 2001. Unfortunately, the Enterprise network waned and Doncaster Belmont closed as a marshalling point in late 2008. (*Paul Shannon*)

If Crewe is the archetypal railway town, then Immingham is the archetypal railway port, developed by the Great Central Railway in the early twentieth century to handle exports of coal and other materials that arrived by rail. One hundred years later, Immingham was still one of the busiest rail freight locations in the UK. While most of the business was moved in full trainloads, the sorting sidings at Immingham handled various wagonload flows during the EWS Enterprise era including paper, containers, steel, zinc ingots and timber. 08689 shunts a short rake of containers on 7 August 2002. (*Paul Shannon*)

The power of nature is all too evident in this photograph of Tinsley dated 3 June 2004. Pilot loco 08528 passes the site of the hump as it propels a rake of steel wagons from one of the two Outokumpu Stainless plants into the rump of the yard. Further transformation would soon take place as the yard site was earmarked for redevelopment as a rail-linked distribution terminal. Unfortunately, the distribution terminal failed to generate any rail traffic, but the west end of the site became an aggregates terminal with regular trains from Leicestershire. (*Paul Shannon*)

Although Tees Yard closed as a marshalling yard in 1993, rail freight activity continued in parts of the former up yard into the twenty-first century. The 12 up staging and departure sidings were retained mainly for eastbound trains, while the larger fan of sidings in the former up hump yard were used by westbound trains. On 11 July 2011, 66034 sets out from the up yard with 6V02, the 1843 departure to Margam, conveying lime containers and empty steel carriers for Port Talbot. Most of the other wagons in the yard at that time were in long term storage. (*Paul Shannon*)

In the Midlands, the yard complex at Toton was geared mainly to wagonload coal, which declined through a combination of lost business and conversion to train-load merry-go-round operation. Its down and up humps closed in 1978 and 1984 respectively. A small fan of sidings has been retained for infrastructure traffic. The main marshalling centre for the West Midlands was Bescot, which ceased to be a hump yard in 1984 but continued to handle general freight and survives today for staging, storage and infrastructure traffic. The smaller yard at Washwood Heath lost much of its work around 1970 but remained in use for local wagonload traffic as well as various trainload flows; it closed completely in 2008.

Whitemoor was for many decades the gateway yard for East Anglia. Its down hump closed in 1974 and its up hump in 1980, but limited marshalling continued until the end of Speedlink in 1991. In recent years, the tracks have returned to Whitemoor in the shape of a local distribution depot for infrastructure traffic, managed by GB Railfreight.

In London and the South East, wagonload shunting was carried out at several locations. Hump shunting at Willesden Sudbury Sidings ceased in 1971, when the work was transferred to the flat shunted Brent yard. In the late 1980s, Willesden Brent was the busiest Speedlink yard on the network. It was largely replaced in 1993 by Wembley European Freight Operating Centre, which will almost certainly prove to be the last marshalling yard built in the UK. For a time, Wembley was busy with Channel Tunnel traffic and various domestic flows, but wagonload activity ceased in 2010 and the sidings are used today as a staging point for trainload traffic. On the east side of the city, Temple Mills lost its hump in 1982 and closed before the end of Speedlink in favour of direct trip workings to and from Willesden. On the west side of London, Acton yard closed in 1984, but the site now houses a large aggregates depot as well as a small fan of sidings for staging.

The flat yard at Crewe Basford Hall became an important base for Freightliner, both as an operating location for intermodal trains and later as a centre for infrastructure traffic. This view dated 27 October 2011 shows a typical range of wagon types and Class 66 locomotives stabled in the yard. On the far right is the virtual quarry for stockpiling railway ballast. (*Paul Shannon*)

Since the demise of wagonload freight, the busiest yards have been those handling railway infrastructure traffic such as ballast, spoil and rails. A case in point is Whitemoor, where Network Rail established an infrastructure base on part of the former marshalling yard site in 2004. GB Railfreight manages all operations at the site. 66701 shunts IOA ballast wagons at the south end of the yard on 26 October 2018, with the abandoned branch to Wisbech visible on the right. (*Paul Shannon*)

South Wales was still busy with wagonload freight in 1970. Most traffic to and from England passed through Severn Tunnel Junction yard, which took on a major role in the Speedlink network from the late 1970s onwards. However, there was less and less need for hump shunting and the down and up humps closed in 1978 and 1982 respectively. Before long, BR decided that it could do without Severn Tunnel Junction altogether: The whole complex closed in 1987 and its functions passed to smaller yards such as Gloucester, East Usk Junction and Cardiff Tidal. On the western side of the South Wales industrial belt, Margam yard lost its hump in 1980 but remained busy; it was replaced in 1987 by the more compact

Margam Knuckle yard, which is still an operating location for steel trains today.

While almost every major yard that existed in 1970 has either disappeared or declined in size and importance, there is still a need for groups of sidings at strategic points on the network. Each operating company has its preferred locations for staging and stabling trains. In South Wales, for example, DB Cargo uses Alexandra Dock Junction yard, while Freightliner tends to use East Usk Junction yard and GB Railfreight uses the sidings alongside the main line at Cardiff Pengam. But it is really only infrastructure traffic that requires yards as such; the mechanised hump yard as conceived in the 1955 Modernisation Plan is well and truly dead.

CHAPTER 5

SIGNALLING AND ELECTRIFICATION

In 1970, traditional signal boxes and mechanical semaphore arms still controlled much of the BR network, not only on secondary routes but also on lengthy stretches of the East Coast main line, the Midland main line and the northern half of the West Coast main line. Gradually, power boxes and Integrated Electronic Control Centres have spread their coverage and the total number of signal boxes on the network has fallen every year. But the age of the semaphore is not yet over: Some pockets of mechanical signalling are expected to survive into the 2030s and occasionally Network Rail replaces semaphore signals on a like for like basis, as happened at Henwick, Worcester, in 2017.

Multiple aspect signalling is nothing new. The Great Central Railway installed three-aspect colour light signals between London Marylebone and Neasden in 1923 and the South Eastern & Chatham Railway went a step further by installing four-aspect signals between Holborn Viaduct and Elephant & Castle in 1926. After the Grouping of 1923, the GWR resignalled several major station areas with colour lights including Paddington, Bristol and Cardiff. The SR installed colour lights on the newly electrified Brighton main line and the LNER modernised a long stretch of the East Coast main line between York and Newcastle.

Mechanical signalling abounds at the north end of Peterborough station on 22 May 1970. Two years later, BR would complete a major remodelling of the station area, eliminating two reverse curves and increasing the maximum speed for non-stop trains from 20mph to 100mph. All the semaphores would go, and fifteen signal boxes on the four-mile stretch between Fletton Junction and Werrington Junction would become redundant. Further change would come to Peterborough with electrification in 1987 and track capacity enhancements in 2013/14, enabling the station to cope better with the mixture of InterCity, cross-country and local trains. (*Neil Caplan/Online Transport Archive*)

GWR-style lower quadrant signals and an ageing water tower set the scene at Borth, near Aberystwyth, as a Class 101 DMU heads for Machynlleth and, eventually, Birmingham New Street in summer 1971. The line had been transferred from the Western to the London Midland Region in 1963 but there was no need to change the signalling. Borth would lose its passing loop and signal box in the 1970s, leaving a 16-mile single track section from Dovey Junction to Aberystwyth. (*R.W.A. Jones/Online Transport Archive*)

The Bidston-Wrexham line was an unlikely outpost of the Eastern Region for a short period after Nationalisation, having previously belonged to the LNER and, before that, the Great Central Railway. The ex-GCR box at Hawarden oversees the passage of a Class 108 DMU bound for Wrexham in spring 1973. The box would close in 1979, reductions in freight traffic having made it possible to extend the block section from Dee Marsh Junction to Penyffordd. (*R.W.A. Jones/ Online Transport Archive*)

The southern end of the Midland main line retained its manual signalling until preparatory work started for electrification. 25277 heads south at Napsbury with an electrification works train on 17 September 1979. The signal box was situated between the down slow and up slow lines because there had been an island platform here until 1959. Co-acting signals were provided in the up direction to ensure visibility from beyond the overbridge. The positioning of the colour light signals on the new gantry in the foreground shows that the up slow would soon be realigned, leaving little evidence of the former station. (*Paul Shannon*)

Many semaphores are in evidence as 47255 enters Ely station with the Harwich-Manchester boat train on 2 June 1980. In the distance it is just possible to make out Ely Dock Junction box, which controlled the divergence of the lines to Cambridge and Bury St Edmunds. The sidings on the right are filled with redundant stock on its way to Snailwell scrapyard. Ely South box closed in June 1985 when its work was transferred to Ely North box at the other end of the station. The main line through Ely was electrified in 1992. (*Paul Shannon*)

In 1980, Exeter St David's came under the control of two boxes, Exeter Middle and Exeter West. Both dated back to the GWR station remodelling carried out in 1912-15. Perched on its slim brick base and tightly sandwiched between two running lines, Exeter Middle box is visible in this scene as 50006 arrives on a down express on 10 June 1980. The semaphores at Exeter would last until the spring of 1985, when Exeter signalling centre was commissioned. At the same time, the track layout was simplified, with fewer points and crossings in order to reduce maintenance costs. (*Paul Shannon*)

This fine gantry of upper quadrant sema-phores at Southampton Central survived until the Southampton area was resignalled in 1981. Electrification had already reached the city in 1967. Class 205 DEMU 1128 sets off from Southampton Central with a Portsmouth-Salisbury train in summer 1980. The signal posts on the gantry were arranged in three groups of three, indicating the three routes available from the bay platform line, the down local line and the down through line. (*Michael Rhodes*)

In the Aberdeen area, six manual signal boxes were abolished in summer 1981 and replaced by a power box which linked up to Newtonhill in the south and Dyce in the north. A single colour light post hints at the impending change as 55007 *Pinza* runs round its train – the 0550 departure from London King's Cross – on 21 March 1981. The box in the distance is Aberdeen South, which controlled three signal gantries and oversaw the access to Clayhills carriage and HST inspection shed. (*Paul Shannon*)

Barrow Hill, on the 'old road' from Chesterfield to Rotherham, boasted a forest of semaphore signals long after the main line into Sheffield was modernised. 46047 passes Barrow Hill Junction box with a down ballast train on 27 July 1981. Originally named Staveley Junction, this Midland Railway box dated back to 1928 and controlled the junction for Seymour as well as movements on the main line. In the distance is Barrow Hill Down Sidings box, of similar Midland design, which controlled the access to Barrow Hill loco depot. The line through Barrow Hill was resignalled in November 1981 when control passed to Sheffield power box. Today, the layout at Barrow Hill has been greatly reduced, although a small fan of sidings is still available for stabling freight trains. (*Paul Shannon*)

The last surviving Great Northern somersault signals on BR were found on the Skegness branch. Nine examples lasted into the 1980s. A five-car DMU formation passes two somersaults as it enters Havenhouse station with a Skegness-Nottingham service on 1 August 1981. Havenhouse box would close in March 1989, when the level crossing lost its gates in favour of automatic half barriers monitored from neighbouring Wainfleet. (*Paul Shannon*)

Although it had lost its glass overall roof in 1975, Mallaig station retained much of its traditional railway atmosphere at the start of the 1980s. The signal box was still fully operational and trains were locomotive-hauled. Fuel oil tanks were attached when required to the evening passenger service from Fort William. On 27 August 1981, 37112 sets back into the station after running round its train. But change was not far away: Mallaig box was converted to a ground frame in March 1982 and all semaphore signals were removed. The signalling system on the line was changed to Radio Electronic Token Block in December 1987, controlled from Banavie signalling centre. The running of mixed passenger and freight trains finished in 1987 when locomotive haulage gave way to Sprinter units. (*Paul Shannon*)

By the mid-1970s, multiple aspect signalling controlled just under half of the total track mileage on BR. It was possible to cover some long distances without encountering a semaphore on the running line, such as from Paddington to Taunton (exclusive), from Paddington to Swansea (exclusive), from Bristol to Birmingham and from Birmingham to Sheffield. But many examples of antiquated signalling survived as well. The London Midland Region had long been upper quadrant territory, but ex-Midland Railway lower quadrant signals survived at various locations including Rufford and Ketton – the latter example lasting extraordinarily into the twenty-first century. Knutsford on the ex-Cheshire Lines Committee line to Chester boasted the last example of a tall lower quadrant shunting signal until it was removed in 1981. The Eastern Region retained a number of somersault signals dating back to Great Northern Railway days. On the Skegness branch alone, nine somersaults survived into the mid-1980s.

Resignalling schemes in the 1970s ranged from the provision of substitute manual boxes still controlling semaphore signals to major projects involving the replacement of dozens of boxes with a single power installation. Examples of new manual boxes were Heysham Harbour in 1970, Penyffordd 1972, Bedford St Johns in 1977, Ravenhead Junction in 1978, Uttoxeter in January 1981 and Porth in March 1981. The small ground level box at Porth was the last new mechanical box built by BR and remained in use until 1998.

At the other end of the scale, the total route modernisation of the northern half of the West Coast main line in the early 1970s led to the work of numerous manual boxes, many dating back to the nineteenth

Of the various overhead signal cabins that once existed between London Waterloo and Clapham Junction, only two – Clapham 'A' and West London Junction – survived into the 1980s. Class 405 units 4656 and 4637 pass under Clapham 'A' with a down suburban service on 21 September 1981. The framework surrounding the box once supported a steel roof that had been erected as an air raid precaution during the Second World War. Clapham 'A' box closed in May 1990 when the area came under the control of Wimbledon power box. (*Paul Shannon*)

The East Coast main line between Durham and Ferryhill was resignalled in 1971, but the North Eastern Railway box at Hett Mill was retained as a gate box until March 1984 when it came under the control of Ferryhill. In 1991, the responsibility passed to Tyneside Integrated Electronic Control Centre. An InterCity 125 unit powered by cars 43070 and 43061 passes Hett Mill on 14 March 1982. By that time, Hett Mill was already the last manned level crossing between York and Newcastle. (*Paul Shannon*)

century, being taken over by just four power boxes at Warrington, Preston, Carlisle and Motherwell. The Preston scheme was interesting because of its wide geographical coverage. It was implemented in ten stages between November 1972 and October 1973 and when complete it covered the West Coast main line from Standish Junction near Wigan to Carnforth, the East Lancashire and Copy Pit lines, and even a stretch of the Calder Valley line between Smithy Bridge and Hebden Bridge. Some 57 manual boxes were made redundant and several more were reduced to gate boxes or shunting frames.

On the East Coast main line, three power installations at King's Cross, Peterborough and Doncaster took over the work of well over 100 boxes, most of them mechanical, between 1971 and 1979. The scheme covered some 160 route miles from King's Cross to Shaftholme Junction, just north of Doncaster. The last East Coast main line semaphore was removed from Doncaster Decoy No 2 box in 1978. Alongside resignalling, the East Coast scheme involved a lot of track layout changes. At King's Cross, the approach tracks were rearranged to segregate main line and suburban traffic and bidirectional working was introduced. At Peterborough, the punishing reverse curves at both ends of the station were straightened out and two new non-platform lines allowed trains to pass through at 100mph instead of 20mph. At Doncaster, a new spur was provided from St Catherine's Junction to Down Decoy, giving trains from the South Yorkshire Joint Line direct access to the down side of the East Coast main line. However, the layout at the south end of Doncaster station became more restricted as the approach from Sheffield was reduced to single track.

Western and London Midland influences are seen side by side at Kensington Olympia, as the down loop and through lines are signalled by lower and upper quadrants respectively. 73102 heads south with an inter-regional transfer freight on 19 April 1982. Signs of rationalisation are already visible, and Kensington North Main box would close in January 1983. Its partner Kensington South Main would survive until October 1992, when control of the line passed to Victoria Signalling Centre. (*Paul Shannon*)

Although it had closed to passengers in 1954, Leyburn station on the Redmire branch retained much of its original track layout for the next 29 years. 47288 passes a rare example of a North Eastern Railway slotted signal as it heads east with 6K13, the 0835 Redmire-Redcar limestone train, on 17 May 1982. At that time there were still nine signal or gate boxes on the branch and the goods yards at Bedale and Leyburn were still open for wagonload coal deliveries. That was all set to change: The coal traffic ceased shortly after the date of the photograph and Leyburn box and loop closed in October 1983. (*Paul Shannon*)

Westbury North box controlled the north – or east – end of the station, including the junction of lines to Bristol and Reading. This fine array of starting signals, with route indicators on two of the posts, allowed a fair amount of routeing flexibility for northbound departures. On 29 July 1982, 33014 arrives with the 1114 from Bristol Temple Meads to Portsmouth Harbour. Westbury North and four other manual boxes were replaced in May 1984 by Westbury power box, whose area was later extended towards Exeter, Bristol, Reading and Salisbury. (*Paul Shannon*)

The last major signal gantry to survive in the Bolton area was at Burnden Junction, where a curve once diverged to meet the Bolton-Rochdale line. A Class 104 formation comprising power cars M53475, M53527, M53473 and M53525 approaches Bolton on an evening service from Manchester Victoria on 4 June 1983. The area was resignalled in December 1985, when Bolton power box replaced the manual boxes at Burnden Junction, Bolton East Junction and Bolton West. The power box in turn closed in January 1990 when control passed to Manchester Piccadilly. (*Paul Shannon*)

The 100-lever Kings Dock Junction signal box controlled an extraordinarily complex layout at the entrance to Swansea Docks. 08400 arrives with a train of coal for export in 1983, still comprising unfitted MDO mineral wagons which were then close to the end of their lives. The box dated back to 1908 and was operated by Associated British Ports. Traffic to the docks declined sharply in the 1980s and the box was taken out of use in 1987, all remaining points being converted to hand operation. (*Michael Rhodes*)

A number of Southern Region lines remained semaphore signalled in the early 1980s. Class 421 EMU 7373 enters Barnham station with a train from Portsmouth on 27 August 1983. The tracks converging from the left are those of the Bognor Regis branch. Barnham signal box closed in November 2008, but that was far from the end of its story. A group called Save Barnham Signal Box Campaign saved the 1911-built structure from demolition and in December 2009 it was moved on a road transporter to a new site at Aldingbourne sports ground. (*Paul Shannon*)

The last section of the Midland main line to lose its semaphore signals was the so-called Leicester gap. 31407 passes an abundance of semaphores as it approaches Leicester station with a Birmingham train on 24 April 1984. BR commissioned the first stage of the Leicester gap resignalling scheme in June 1986, and by December 1987 Leicester power box controlled the whole line from Sharnbrook to Loughborough, linking up with West Hampstead power box in the south and Trent power box in the north. (*Paul Shannon*)

The resignalling of the Midland main line took rather longer to complete. The first 50 miles of the route from London St Pancras to Bedford were resignalled between October 1979 and November 1980 in preparation for electrification. But the so-called Leicester Gap from Sharnbrook to Loughborough was not plugged until December 1987, when Leicester power box was fully commissioned. The Leicester scheme abolished 24 manual boxes and, more controversially, it removed more than 40 miles of superfluous track, a target achieved mainly by reducing the formation from four tracks to three between Sharnbrook and Harrowden, from four tracks to two between Harrowden and Kettering and from two tracks to one between Kettering and Corby. A third track between Harrowden and Kettering would be restored in 2009 and work was under way to reinstate missing tracks on the other sections in 2018.

On the Western Region, multiple aspect signalling gradually extended westwards. The Westbury area was resignalled from May 1984 onwards, eventually taking over the work of 16 mechanical boxes and joining up with areas controlled from Reading, Salisbury, Bristol and Exeter. Exeter power box was commissioned in stages between March 1985 and December 1987, by which time there were no semaphores left between Paddington and Plymouth.

In Scotland, two significant schemes took place during the 1970s and early 1980s. One was focused on Edinburgh and saw the abolition of more than 60 mechanical boxes between 1976 and 1980, stretching from Berwick-on-Tweed to Thornton on the East Coast route and including several lines in the Central Belt. A smaller but important scheme saw Aberdeen power box take over the work of six manual boxes in 1981.

Marking a remote spot on the Ayr-Stranraer line, Glenwhilly station closed to goods in 1964 and passengers in 1965, but the box and loop remained in use to break what would otherwise have been an 18-mile stretch of single track between Barrhill and Dunragit. 27014 slows for the token exchange at Glenwhilly with the 1S40 London Euston to Stranraer parcels train on 25 July 1985. On the left is an example of the tablet picking-up and setting-down apparatus which was once common at the beginning and end of single-track sections. (*Paul Shannon*)

Scenes like this have been a regular sight on Britain's railways for many a decade as nineteenth century technology has gradually given way to automation. One of the gantries south of Bolton station is in the process of being denuded on a misty 8 December 1985. As well as removing the semaphores, BR took the opportunity to simplify the track layout through Bolton station, with all trains to and from the Blackburn being routed via the island platform on the up side. Further remodelling would take place in 2017 as part of the Manchester-Preston electrification scheme. (*Paul Shannon*)

Since the 1990s resignalling has continued apace with a mixture of large and small schemes, often lagging behind schedule but nonetheless slowly working towards the aim of eliminating nineteenth century signalling practice from Britain's railways. In recent years resignalling has meant not only the abolition of mechanical boxes but also the closure of relatively recent power boxes. The work of Leicester and Trent power boxes, for example, was subsumed into the East Midlands Control Centre at Derby in 2011 and 2013 respectively.

On lightly used lines, BR introduced Radio Electronic Token Block signalling in the 1980s, enabling the removal of signals and signal boxes without the expense of replacing them with new fixed installations and many miles of cabling. The Kyle of Lochalsh line was the guinea pig for RETB with a six-month trial in 1984; the system was a success and by the end of the decade it had been introduced to the Far North line to Wick and Thurso, the West Highland lines to Oban and Mallaig, the Cambrian lines from Shrewsbury to Aberystwyth and Pwllheli, and the East Suffolk line from Ipswich to Lowestoft. RETB was replaced by the European Rail Traffic Management System on the Cambrian lines in 2011 and was phased out on the East Suffolk line in 2012 but has remained in use in an updated form on the Scottish routes.

Pockets of semaphore signalling survived on secondary lines in London long after the modernisation of the main radial routes. The Midland Railway box at Leytonstone High Road on the Gospel Oak-Barking line oversees the arrival of a Class 104 DMU comprising cars 53437 and 53479 on 28 October 1987. The box was taken out of use in January 1993 and closed in February 1994. The first-generation DMUs on the Gospel Oak-Barking line were later replaced by more reliable Class 150 units, which in turn gave way to Class 172 Turbostar units. However, the biggest improvement will come from electrification, which was finally authorised in 2013. (*Paul Shannon*)

The open ground frame at Millbrook, on the Bedford-Bletchley line, was an extraordinary survivor from the early days of the LNWR, when some stations had no proper signal box as such. The frame at Millbrook had originally been completely open to the elements but gained a Perspex roof in 1990. This scene from 1 January 1994 also shows the small hut that accommodated the signaller. Modernisation finally came to the Bedford-Bletchley line in September 2004 when a new signalling control centre at Ridgmont opened. The line is likely to be upgraded further as part of the East West Rail route, although plans to electrify it have been shelved. (*Paul Shannon*)

An anachronism in the 1990s was Willesborough crossing just east of Ashford. It was the last manned level crossing on the main line from Dover to London, the local topography making it difficult to replace it with a bridge. 47292 passes Willesborough with 6M86, the 0855 Dover to Crewe train, on 14 February 1994. This was a wagonload service conveying traffic from the Dunkerque-Dover train ferry, traffic which would soon be using the Channel Tunnel. The level crossing was finally replaced by an underpass for pedestrians and cyclists in April 2001, in conjunction with the building of HS1 alongside the classic route. (*Paul Shannon*)

The very last example of a Great Northern Railway somersault signal guards this level crossing on the Boston Docks branch, although judging by the closed gates, its aspect should not be taken too literally. The unusual octagonal box also controls movements over the late nineteenth century swing bridge into the docks, located behind the photographer. Rail traffic to and from Boston Docks declined sharply in the 1970s and 1980s and ceased altogether between 1993 and 1997, but since then there have been regular trainloads of imported steel bound for the West Midlands. (*Paul Shannon*)

Attleborough was one of nine manual signal boxes which closed with the resignalling of the Norwich to Ely line in December 2012. The 1886-built Great Eastern Railway structure and traditional crossing gates – albeit with a modern CCTV camera – were still in use on 21 November 2010 when unit 170207 was photographed on a Norwich to Cambridge working. Once the resignalling was complete, the gates were replaced by automatic barriers with obstacle detectors, a system that was also adopted between Shrewsbury and Crewe. (*Paul Shannon*)

The signalling on the Oxford-Leamington Spa line was renewed piecemeal over several decades. The demise of the last two manual boxes on the route, Banbury North and Banbury South, finally became reality in August 2016. Approaching Banbury station on 19 August 2013 is Chiltern Railways unit 168215 on a service to London Marylebone. The area is now controlled from West Midlands signalling centre at Saltley, with a revised track layout allowing greater flexibility for the increased number of passenger trains using the route. (*Paul Shannon*)

The last example on Network Rail of a Lancashire & Yorkshire Railway all-timber box with its original frame was Ashton Moss North Junction. It controlled an island of semaphore signals on the Manchester Victoria to Stalybridge line, where the freight-only line from Stockport via Denton converged from the south. Unit 156428 passes the junction on 16 April 2014 with a stopping train to Huddersfield. The gantry on the left is a relic of the time when a branch of the electrified Woodhead system extended to Ashton Moss. The area was resignalled in April 2018. (*Paul Shannon*)

The Midland Railway box at St Albans was grade II listed in 1979, shortly before its closure as part of the West Hampstead power signalling scheme in 1980. It was left to decay for two decades, but a trust was formed in 2003 to lease the box from Network Rail and since 2008 it has been regularly opened to the public as a museum. Today, the box still sits in its original position, although the railway around it has changed greatly with the removal of crossovers and sidings, electrification and lengthened platforms. Eight-car Thameslink unit 700029 heads south on 26 February 2018. (*Paul Shannon*)

The closure of the Woodhead route in 1981 brought an end to electric-hauled freight trains to the three Yorkshire destinations of Rotherwood, Wath and Tinsley. The electrification covered many sidings as well as running lines, especially at Wath which was the main gathering point for coal traffic over the Pennines. 76049 departs from Wath yard with a train conveying mainly household coal for Lancashire on 15 April 1980. At that time there were still up to a dozen electric-hauled departures from Wath each weekday, most of them bound for Fiddlers Ferry. (*Paul Shannon*)

Although Network Rail announced plans in August 2011 to concentrate railway signalling in 14 rail operating control centres, this is clearly a long-term aspiration. In the meantime, the attractiveness of many traditional signal boxes has not gone unnoticed. More than 150 of the structures have been listed for their architectural and historical interest, ranging from a selection of early pre-Grouping boxes to the 1964 power installation at Birmingham New Street. Many are no longer in railway use and a few have been restored, a notable example being St Albans South which still stands in its original position and houses a fascinating museum.

The electrification of Britain's railways has been a long, and often interrupted, process. In 1970, much of the Southern Region was already electrified on the 650-750V dc third rail system, as were some lines on Merseyside and out of London Euston and Broad Street, while overhead wires provided 25kV or 6.25kV ac power to the southern half of the West Coast main line, suburban lines around Glasgow and various routes to the north and east of London. There were also some non-standard systems, notably 1,500V dc overhead on the Woodhead route and the Manchester-Altrincham line, and 1,200V dc side-contact third rail on the Manchester-Bury line.

The non-standard systems were gradually phased out. The Manchester-Altrincham line was converted to 25kV in 1971 and the western end of the former Woodhead route was similarly converted in 1984. The

Bury line kept its unique side contact system until it closed for conversion to Metrolink operation in 1991.

The biggest electrification scheme to be completed in the 1970s was the extension of 25kV overhead from Weaver Junction to Glasgow. The best London to Glasgow journey time was cut to five hours from May 1974 and many heavy freight trains also benefited from electric haulage over Shap and Beattock banks. In London and the South East, the long-awaited Great Northern electric project came to fruition, reaching Welwyn Garden City and Hertford in 1976 and Royston two years later. The inner suburban trains were dual voltage so that they could run on the third rail section between Finsbury Park and Moorgate as well as on the 25kV overhead lines elsewhere. On Merseyside, the third rail system was extended to the new Liverpool link and loop lines and out to Kirkby and Garston.

Many more electrification schemes were completed during the 1980s, mostly 25kV overhead but with some extensions to existing third rail networks as well. Electric trains between Moorgate and Bedford finally started running in March 1983, with a full service launched in January 1984. This scheme paved the way for Thameslink later in the decade, with its dual voltage trains providing new through routes across the capital. Several extensions were completed to the north and east of London, with the wires reaching Norwich, Harwich and Cambridge in 1987. Outer suburban schemes included Romford-Upminster, Wickford-Southminster and Watford Junction-St Albans Abbey, the first and last of these having fought back from the threat of closure twenty years earlier.

The East Coast main line in transition is pictured on 19 August 1988, as 56133 heads south at Thirsk with a trainload of containerised coal from Lynemouth to Ellesmere Port. The masts would soon sprout catenary and the wires would be energised as far as Northallerton in June 1990. Thirsk signal box, which dated back to an earlier resignalling scheme in the 1930s, would be abolished in January 1990 when control of the line passed to York Integrated Electronic Control Centre. Full electric operation to Edinburgh would begin in June 1991. (*Paul Shannon*)

The 6½-mile 'Abbey line' from Watford Junction to St Albans Abbey was electrified at 25kV ac in July 1988, eliminating a diesel-operated offshoot from the long-electrified West Coast main line. Initially the electric service used dual voltage Class 313 units, of the same type that ran on the third-rail system between London Euston, Watford Junction and Croxley Green. Unit 313005 stands at the terminus on 28 August 1988 before departing with the 1722 service to Watford Junction. Various proposals have been made to improve the service and, in particular, to increase its frequency from the minimum 45-minute interval dictated by the lack of an intermediate passing loop. So far, the costs of any improvement have been judged to be prohibitive. (*Paul Shannon*)

The wires finally reached Cambridge in late 1986 and a full electric service to London Liverpool Street was launched in May 1987. For a time, passengers enjoyed the luxury of Class 86 haulage, although in railway operating terms this was awkward, because through trains to and from King's Lynn had to change traction at Cambridge. It would be another five years before the electrification stretched to King's Lynn. On 26 May 1988, 86259 departs from Cambridge with the 1410 King's Lynn to Liverpool Street train. The mixture of livery styles is typical of that era, with an InterCity locomotive hauling Network SouthEast and BR blue and grey coaches. (*Paul Shannon*)

The North London line through Camden Road has seen several changes in its electric operation. The LNWR installed third (and fourth) rail electrification on the route in 1916 for local passenger trains. BR added overhead wires to the freight lines in 1965 for Freightliner traffic to Maiden Lane, but this operation only lasted a few years. A second, more ambitious wiring scheme was completed in February 1988 when 25kV ac electrification catered for through freight traffic between the West Coast main line and the Great Eastern main line. Local passenger services at that time continued to use the third rail system. However, by 2010 the third rail through Camden Road had been removed, with both freight and passenger trains using the overhead wires. On 4 November 1988, Class 416 unit 6316 passes Camden Road with an eastbound service. (*Paul Shannon*)

Most electrification schemes since the mid-twentieth century have targeted passenger rather than freight traffic. An exception was the West Coast main line, which was conceived as a mixed traffic scheme from its beginnings in the late 1950s to the fulfilment of wiring to Glasgow in 1974. Even then, there has been an increasing trend to running diesel traction under the wires, for passenger as well as freight trains. One train that enjoyed electric haulage for several years was the flow of clay slurry from Antwerp via the Channel Tunnel. 92013 is about to tackle the 1 in 75 climb to Shap as it passes Greenholme with 6S94, the 0443 from Wembley to Irvine, on 13 February 2008. (*Paul Shannon*)

Most Freightliner trains on the Great Eastern main line between Stratford and Ipswich went over to electric haulage once the North London line was wired up. However, the scheme has its limitations; any electric trains have to change traction at Ipswich yard because the Felixstowe branch is not electrified, and some trains to and from Felixstowe use the non-electrified route via Ely because of limited capacity on the Great Eastern. 90049 crosses the River Stour at Manningtree with 4M81, the 0734 Freightliner train from Felixstowe North to Widnes, on 9 April 2010. (*Paul Shannon*)

On the Southern Region, third rail electrification reached Hastings, East Grinstead, Weymouth and the Portsmouth-Southampton line, helping to reduce the number of diesel-worked pockets on the network and hastening the demise of the Southern DEMU fleet. The Hastings project included singling the track through three of the line's narrow tunnels, which had previously required special stock.

The North London line benefited from two electrification systems: The third rail was extended from Dalston to Stratford and North Woolwich for suburban trains and overhead wires were installed between Camden and Stratford for freight traffic. The latter scheme was very much an exception to the pattern of passenger-orientated electrification: On most newly electrified routes,

freight trains would remain diesel-hauled to avoid the cost and complexity of locomotive changes en route.

Towards the end of the decade, the big project was the wiring up of the East Coast main line. Electric trains reached Leeds in 1988, York in 1989 and Edinburgh in 1991. BR also took the opportunity to electrify the Carstairs-Edinburgh line, providing a through link between the West and East Coast routes and the first electrified route between Edinburgh and Glasgow – of which there are now four! Some provision was made for electrically hauled freight trains on the East Coast main line, but it was scarcely used.

The 1990s brought a lull in major electrification schemes, but there were still a few additions to the network, including extensions to the third rail Merseyrail

On the East Coast main line, the electric haulage of freight trains has been very limited. For a time, the flow of steel from Scunthorpe to Ébange was electric-hauled south of Doncaster, although it has since reverted to diesel traction throughout. On 25 June 2011, 92007 heads north at Marholm with 4E32, the 1155 empties from Dollands Moor to Scunthorpe. On this stretch the down Stamford line doubles up as the down slow line for the East Coast route, hence the uneven pattern of electrified tracks. (*Paul Shannon*)

The eight-mile route between Crewe and Kidsgrove was electrified in 2003, mainly for use as a diversionary route while the West Coast main line was being upgraded. London Midland then introduced a regular electric service over the line in 2008. Unit 350130 heads east near Barthomley with a train from Crewe to London Euston via Stoke-on-Trent on 26 May 2012. The three-mile stretch between Crewe and Barthomley was singled in 1985; Network Rail considered redoubling it, but the cost could not be justified. (*Paul Shannon*)

system, the wiring of the once threatened lines to Ilkley and Skipton, and the Birmingham cross-city line from Redditch to Lichfield. In 1998, the launch of Heathrow Express saw the first electric trains using London Paddington – at which point Marylebone became the only non-electrified London terminus.

In the twenty-first century, new third rail schemes have been conspicuous by their absence and there have even been suggestions that some third rail lines might be converted to overhead, partly for improved efficiency and partly for safety reasons. Meanwhile, the overhead network has continued to grow, albeit at a slower rate than planned. The two-stage opening of HS1 brought overhead electrification to the former Southern Region on a scale not seen before. Several lines in the Central Belt of Scotland have been electrified, with more to come. In North West England, routes from Manchester to Liverpool and Blackpool have been wired and a start has been made on electrifying the Great Western main line, although it is not yet clear how far the catenary will stretch. Both on the Great Western and on the Midland main line, the rise of bi-modal traction may turn out to be a double-edged sword, on the one hand allowing more trains to run on electric power when under the wires but on the other hand making extensions of the electrified network less worthwhile.

Local lines into Glasgow have been progressively electrified since the first stretch of the North Clyde network went live in 1960. In recent years, the focus has been on lines to the east and north of the city. The ten-mile line between Springburn and Cumbernauld switched to electric operation in May 2014, allowing trains on that route to run through to Dumbarton via Glasgow Queen Street Low Level. ScotRail unit 334025 passes Greenfoot on an afternoon service from Cumbernauld on 7 August 2014. (*Paul Shannon*)

The electrification of the Great Western main line began with the launch of Heathrow Express in June 1998. A more affordable but slower service between London Paddington and Heathrow was introduced in 2005, using Class 360 Desiro EMUs and marketed as Heathrow Connect. Pulling away from West Ealing with a Heathrow-bound train on 18 February 2018 is unit 360201. As part of the major Great Western electrification scheme electric trains would reach Maidenhead in May 2017 and Didcot in January 2018. (*Paul Shannon*)

After closure of the Woodhead route, the venerable Class 506 units remained in operation between Hadfield and Manchester for several years, but BR then converted the line to 25kV ac operation in order to replace worn-out equipment and make the line compatible with the rest of the South Manchester network. The changeover took place in December 1984. Several types of electric unit have plied the line since then. Unit 323223 recedes past Hyde Junction with a train from Hadfield via Glossop on 24 October 2016. (*Paul Shannon*)

Electrification to Chester was achieved in 1993 thanks to an extension of the third rail from Hooton. This gave Chester its first regular trains to Liverpool since the downgrading of the Frodsham-Runcorn curve in the 1970s. Unit 507007 approaches Chester with a morning train from Liverpool (technically from Chester to Chester via the Liverpool loop) on 29 November 2016. In the background is the Alstom depot which replaced the earlier shed pictured on page 119 (*Paul Shannon*)

The electrification of the Great Western main line has been beset by delays, deferrals and part-cancellation. However, the use of bi-mode technology will at least allow trains to places such as Bristol and Swansea to run under electric power for part of their journey. Running in diesel mode, a pair of Class 800 InterCity Express Train units passes Uffington on the 0900 Bristol Temple Meads-London Paddington service on 14 May 2018. (*Paul Shannon*)

The wiring through Bolton finally went live in 2018, enabling electric units to take over most services on the Manchester-Preston-Blackpool axis. Former Thameslink unit 319376 departs from Bolton with the 0704 Preston-Manchester Victoria train on 3 July 2019. (*Paul Shannon*)

MAIN ELECTRIFICATION SCHEMES COMPLETED SINCE 1970		
1974	Weaver Jn-Glasgow	
1976	Moorgate/King's Cross-Hertford/Welwyn GC	part 3rd rail
1977	Witham-Braintree	
1977	Kirkdale-Kirkby	3rd rail
1978	Hertford/Welwyn GC-Royston	
1978	Sandhills-Liverpool Central-Garston	3rd rail
1981	Mossend-Coatbridge	
1981	Stockport-Hazel Grove	
1983	London St Pancras/Moorgate-Bedford	
1983	Garston-Hunts Cross	3rd rail
1985	Dalston-Stratford-North Woolwich	3rd rail
1985	Colchester-Ipswich	
1985	Rock Ferry-Hooton	3rd rail
1986	Tonbridge-Hastings	3rd rail
1986	Romford-Upminster	
1986	Wickford-Southminster	
1986	Manningtree-Harwich	
1986	Hitchin-Huntingdon	
1986	Paisley-Ayr/Ardrossan	
1987	Ardrossan-Largs	
1987	Bishops Stortford-Cambridge	
1987	Huntingdon-Peterborough	
1987	Ipswich-Norwich	
1987	Sanderstead-East Grinstead	3rd rail
1988	Bournemouth-Weymouth	3rd rail
1988	Royston-Cambridge	
1988	Watford-St Albans Abbey	
1988	Farringdon-Blackfriars (Thameslink)	3rd rail
1988	Peterborough-Leeds	
1989	Doncaster-York	
1989	Carstairs-Edinburgh	
1989	Camden-Stratford	
1990	Portsmouth-Southampton/Eastleigh	3rd rail
1991	York-Edinburgh	
1991	North Berwick branch	
1992	Cambridge-King's Lynn	
1993	North Pole Jn-Kensington-Clapham Jn	3rd rail
1993	Redditch-Birmingham-Lichfield	
1993	Hooton-Chester	3rd rail
1994	Hooton-Ellesmere Port	3rd rail
1994	Leeds/Bradford-Skipton/Ilkley	
1995	Ilkley branch	
1996	Acton Central-Camden Road	changed from 3rd rail to overhead

1998	London Paddington-Heathrow	
2003	Crewe-Kidsgrove	
2003	Channel Tunnel-Fawkham Jn (HS1)	
2007	Ebbsfleet-London St Pancras (HS1)	
2010	Airdrie-Bathgate	
2012	Corkerhill-Paisley Canal	
2014	Springburn/Coatbridge-Cumbernauld	
2014	Rutherglen-Whifflet	
2017	Manchester-Earlestown-Liverpool	
2017	Glasgow-Falkirk-Edinburgh	
2017	Stockley Jn-Reading-Didcot	
2018	Walsall-Rugeley	
2018	Manchester-Bolton-Preston	
2018	Preston-Blackpool North	
2018	Carmuirs-Stirling-Dunblane/Alloa	
2018	Cumbernauld-Greenhill	
2018	Gospel Oak-Barking	
2018	Barnt Green-Bromsgrove	
2018	Didcot-Swindon	
2019	Grangemouth branch	
2019	Holytown-Shotts-Midcalder Jn	

BIBLIOGRAPHY

ALLEN D. and WOOLSTENHOLMES C.J., *A Pictorial Survey of Railway Signalling*, OPC, 1991.

BAKER S.K., *Rail Atlas of Great Britain and Ireland*, various editions, OPC.

British Rail Track Diagrams, various volumes and dates, Quail Map Company.

Rail, *Railways Illustrated* and *Branch Line News*, various issues.

RHODES M., *From Gridiron to Grassland: The Rise and Fall of Britain's Railway Marshalling Yards*, Platform 5, 2016.

THOMAS D. St J. and WHITEHOUSE P., *BR in the Eighties*, David and Charles, 1990.

Petroleum traffic has declined steadily in the last few decades and many rail-fed distribution terminals have closed. Bucking the trend is Colnbrook, where the terminal gained a new lease of life when Freightliner won a long-term contract trains to deliver aviation fuel from Grain. 66610 is about to set back on to its train of empties before departing with 6O00, the 0941 from Colnbrook to Grain, on 1 April 2019. (*Paul Shannon*)

INDEX OF LOCATIONS